'The *Autism Spectrum Guide to Sexuality and Relationships* is a solid guide... Powerful, easy-to-read and practical advice providing knowledge and strategies for people with autism.'

– *Ioannis Voskopoulos and Labrini Ioannou, Psychologists*

of related interest

**Marriage and Lasting Relationships with Asperger's
Syndrome (Autism Spectrum Disorder)**
Successful Strategies for Couples or Counselors
Eva A. Mendes
ISBN 978 1 84905 999 2
eISBN 978 0 85700 981 4

**Asperger Syndrome (Autism Spectrum
Disorder) and Long-Term Relationships**
Fully Revised and Updated with DSM-5® Criteria, Second Edition
Ashley Stanford
ISBN 978 1 84905 773 8
eISBN 978 1 78450 036 8

Troubleshooting Relationships on the Autism Spectrum
A User's Guide to Resolving Relationship Problems
Ashley Stanford
ISBN 978 1 84905 951 0
eISBN 978 0 85700 808 4

The Aspie Girl's Guide to Being Safe with Men
The Unwritten Safety Rules No-one is Telling You
Debi Brown
ISBN 978 1 84905 354 9
eISBN 978 0 85700 703 2

Decoding Dating
**A Guide to the Unwritten Social Rules of Dating for Men
with Asperger Syndrome (Autism Spectrum Disorder)**
John Miller
ISBN 978 1 84905 780 6
eISBN 978 1 78450 040 5

Been There. Done That. Try This!
An Aspie's Guide to Life on Earth
Edited by Tony Attwood, Craig R. Evans and Anita Lesko
ISBN 978 1 84905 964 0
eISBN 978 0 85700 871 8

THE AUTISM SPECTRUM GUIDE TO SEXUALITY AND RELATIONSHIPS

Understand Yourself and Make Choices that are Right for You

Dr Emma Goodall

Forewords by Dr Wenn Lawson and Jeanette Purkis

Jessica Kingsley *Publishers*
London and Philadelphia

First published in 2016
by Jessica Kingsley Publishers
73 Collier Street
London N1 9BE, UK
and
400 Market Street, Suite 400
Philadelphia, PA 19106, USA

www.jkp.com

Library of Congress Cataloging in Publication Data
A CIP catalog record for this book is available from the Library of Congress

British Library Cataloguing in Publication Data
A CIP catalogue record for this book is available from the British Library

ISBN 978 1 84905 705 9
eISBN 978 1 78450 226 3

Printed and bound in Great Britain

This book came about because I have been given the gift of knowledge and an awareness that it really is OK to be yourself, whoever that might be. Many thanks to Jane, who taught me to 'seek to understand', Brian who helped me understand that you can't change the past but you can influence the future by liking yourself and just being yourself, and finally Ben, Mike and Vicki for their influence on my journey.

DISCLAIMER

This book is intended for informational purposes only, and is in no way intended to be a substitute for professional medical advice. The reader should always consult a doctor on matters relating to his/her health.

CONTENTS

FOREWORD

Dr Wenn Lawson

Sexuality and gender identity are different. Both can be quite fluid in a non-binary way allowing us to discover, over time, who we really are. Learning to be comfortable with oneself and with others is a journey that is fraught with difficulty, confusion, misunderstanding and potential for abuse. This brilliant book helps its readers avoid so many of those potential potholes that are waiting along the way.

Being human in all of its many guises has not, in the past, come with a guidebook exploring sexuality and relationships in such broad terminology as this book does. Yet, sexuality and how we understand it in relation to 'self' and 'other' is at the very heart of being human. These two things impact upon who we are, how we relate, and in what ways we enjoy our humanity like nothing else can. Maybe it's because they are so fundamental that we so often fail to talk about these in such broad terms? Maybe we are threatened by such openness, honesty and reality?

In the past (before this book) there have been attempts to address these human attributes. There are umpteen blogs, websites, personal stories even documentaries that tell us the importance of understanding this aspect of our humanity. Yet, not one guide that hosts so many of the needed information; the 'Rights', the possibilities, the 'therefore' and the 'wrong way – turn back', necessary instruction has existed before now.

This book is more than a useful guide to sexuality and relationships in autism, it's a message to us all. Wherever you live on the human spectrum, this book has appropriate information and practical application for you.

Being autistic has meant for so many of us that we have been denied the opportunities that non-autistic individuals enjoy. For some of us, if we expressed our sexuality, we were reprimanded and treated as though this was not a normal human need. So often we ended up in inappropriate situations because no one had helped us to explore with appropriate understanding the things we needed to know. Over time, some of us became resistant to 'being told' and simply continued to get things wrong.

The written word is not the only medium for the sharing of information and practical strategies. Perhaps a carer, parent or professional would need to read this book first, then find ways to relay the appropriate knowledge and knowhow to the person they are sharing it with. Stories have helped humans understand their nature, their needs and the needs of others for all-time. But these stories often need updating and uploading in ways that fit the current generation with its increased sense of awareness and insight. This book is beautifully written. It enables us to take its contents and place them into the right format to make it accessible to others who might not find it easy to relate to the written word. As we create the picture postcards and snapshots in visual, auditory or kinaesthetic format, we truly make it possible for all to benefit.

Over the decades sexual dis-ease and sexual diseases have ruled our history. Domestic violence, and abusive and unequal work relationships have led to many feeling powerless and despairing. This book offers the right advice and practical input to help us choose differently. As autistic people or otherwise, this book has clear instruction on the complete humanity of sexuality and relationships.

The other day a parent asked me when their son would realize that he needed to settle into his being male or female, they didn't mind which, but his moving between the two was causing friction and frustration within the family. I gave the parent an answer they hadn't expected. 'You know, for some of us there is no settling into one or the other, we are both on different days.' I love this quote:

> I've recently been making exciting and very daunting discoveries about my gender. As a result, I currently identify as 30% 'George Clooney' and 70% 'Georgina Clueless'. I'm frantically researching all the posh names for where I'm at and I'm guessing that I'm non-binary/genderqueer with a degree of gender fluidity. Essentially, I live on Planet Drew, which has an erratic rotation around the Gender System. We're currently quite close to Venus. I'm an adult fan of Lego, a sci-fi geek, Doctor Who fan and the occasional gamer. I've also discovered that I can 'do' liquid eyeliner, which is nice! (Planet Drew n.d.)

Coming to terms with the differing ways of being a sexual or non-sexual being with a firm (binary) or non-binary gender expression isn't easy for anyone. Yet, these are all legitimate expressions of humanity. It's time we learnt to not only live and let live, but to welcome and celebrate these differing expressions of who we each are.

Relationships can be tricky for us all. Knowing what love feels like and how to be a real friend or lover is so important. For many autistic people this awareness and insight has been illusive. Our tendency to be loyal, trustworthy and literal has meant many of us end up in poor quality relationships, inappropriate relationships or not in any type of relationship simply because we have lacked the knowhow to understand what it is we need. Then there is the difficulty with interpreting the signs and signals that others are giving out. We may think because someone borrows our stuff, they are our friend. Or, if they introduce themselves to us, that they like us. But these are incomplete scenarios. There are so many reasons why a person may do the above. This book helps us appreciate what a real friend looks like; what an equal relationship feels like; and how we can learn to listen to our body, emotions and feelings, so we can tell the difference.

If I had read a book like this one or if someone else had and then shared the information appropriately with me, I might have been spared some of my life confusion and turmoil. I clumsily fell into many of the potholes this book exposes. Why risk learning the hard way? Why risk the pain and possible dis-ease or disease that ignorance can breed? Why risk living as a second rate citizen just because you didn't know there was any other way to be? Why stay in a broken relationship when there is a way to move on, once you recognize it? An enlightened counsellor once told me: 'Wenn, you stink! You are carrying a dead relationship like a corpse upon your back. The only way to rid yourself of this loathsome and back breaking burden, is to bury this corpse. You can do this by giving it a respectable funeral, which in other terms is called "a divorce".'

When I married as a very young 20-year-old, I had no idea what 'being in love' truly felt like. No idea of what being treated as an equal felt or looked like. And no idea that being emotionally and physically abused and used was *not* OK. Over many years as it became clear the marriage was not based upon a sure foundation of legitimate and appropriate footings, it became obvious to others the relationship was dead. My wedding vows had included such words as: 'until death do us part' – I came to know that death isn't only of a physical nature but can be emotional and mental too. This book helps us to understand how to build a life in the way that works best for us. It also helps us to understand what to do when this is not working for us.

I cannot recommend this book highly enough. Please, do yourself a favour and don't miss out on this most necessary and needed information on sexuality and relationships in autism.

Dr Wenn Lawson

References

Planet Drew (n.d.) About. https://planetdrew.wordpress.com/about, accessed on 15 October 2015.

FOREWORD

Jeanette Purkis

Sexuality, love and relationships form a significant part of life for many people, including those on the autism spectrum. Autistic people have the same sorts of sexual and intimacy needs as others do. They can have all the different sexualities and gender identities that non-autistic adults can have. Despite this, a lot of the resource material about autism and sexuality reads almost like sex education resources for school students. All too often in life and literature, autistic people are cast as sexless, childlike beings. In fact, this could not be further from the truth. We experience the same sorts of attractions and interest in others that non-autistic people do. *The Autism Spectrum Guide to Sexuality and Relationships* addresses this by providing a highly useful guide for adults on the autism spectrum, which focuses on practically everything related to relationships, dating and sex. The book is a refreshingly frank and comprehensive look at a vast range of issues around relationships and sexuality. It is a practical book, filled with useful information about the 'hidden curriculum' of relationships and sex. I would have found this book particularly helpful when I was a young adult coming to terms with my gender identity and sexuality and starting to have my first experiences of sexual relationships.

The book is completely free of any kind of judgement or moralizing. It is respectful and inclusive of the various sexualities and gender differences that people have. Writing from her own autistic perspective, Dr Goodall has delivered a valuable guide to friendships, dating and sexual relationships. The book includes detailed information on a number of topics that autistic adults will find useful, such as different types of sexuality, starting relationships, dating, sexual pleasure and ending relationships. The author provides a comprehensive survey of types of relationships people can experience from casual relationships to long-term relationships and marriage. There is also a very helpful section in the book about having children and how this can impact on the relationships between partners. The text is subtle and nuanced, providing information on some complex topics such as people whose sexuality changes over time and how that can impact on their partner. Few topics are left out, so it really is a one-stop-shop for adults on the spectrum wanting to gather some useful strategies and understanding around the topic of relationships.

This is a great book. I really enjoyed reading it and learned a lot. I think a lot of autistic adults will be assisted by this book as they navigate the often challenging and confusing world of sexuality and relationships.

Jeanette Purkis
– Autism advocate, public speaker, author of Finding a Different Kind of Normal *and* The Wonderful World of Work

INTRODUCTION

While working as an autistic autism spectrum consultant, I found that I was being increasingly asked about resources for autistic adults around friendships, relationships and sexuality. Families and individuals said they couldn't find books that adequately explained how to understand the difference between good relationships and bad, which was extremely problematic as so many autism spectrum adults stay in situations that are not healthy or pleasant because they do not understand that it is not their fault the relationship is not working.

On a personal level, I know that the level of gender and sexual divergence in the autistic community is higher than in the rest of society, and yet there are no resources written for gender questioning or non-heterosexual autistics. This book is designed to introduce autism spectrum adults to the complex world of relationships, gender and sexuality in a non-judgemental and easy-to-understand format. Real-life examples will help readers to understand the variety of experiences and identities and the fluidity of relationships.

As a young adult, I made many of the same relationship mistakes that other adults on the autism spectrum make, and I hope that this book will help readers to avoid some of those mistakes and be able to have more positive and happy relationships of all kinds. Information about family relationships, friendships, sexual and non-sexual relationships is presented. Bad relationships are explored in depth to help people to recognize and therefore prevent these. When it is too late to prevent a bad relationship, safe steps to ending the relationship are given.

Ideas on how to meet people for friendships or relationships are given, along with suggestions on how to maintain these in a positive way. Long-term relationships require a lot of work, and areas of importance to relationships such as money, housing and children are discussed in terms of how this can impact on you and your relationship. In contrast, explanations on how to recognize when people are not really your friend or are treating you badly are given and followed by ways to end relationships.

In recognition that autism spectrum adults are adults with the same range of gender and sexuality as other adults, information on dating, flirting and sex are presented across online and real-life situations for all genders and sexualities. The book starts with a brief overview and then introduces the diversity of gender and sexuality. This is followed by an exploration of the different types of relationships that exist: co-workers, friends, boyfriend/girlfriend, short-term, casual, serious and long-term sexual relationships, marriage and partnerships and family relationships. Within these different relationships, expected behaviours and interpretations of behaviour are explored and illustrated with examples to help the reader to develop and maintain the skills to enjoy a range of positive relationships in the way that suits them best.

Sexuality can be difficult to explain and even more difficult to recognize within yourself for many autism spectrum adults, so the book details how to recognize sexual attraction and the different types of sexuality in yourself and others. The fluidity and diversity of sexuality is illustrated with real-life examples from autism spectrum adults and/or their partners to help readers' identification and understanding of the complexity of sexuality.

Both sexual and non-sexual relationships are explored and explained in a practical manner. This includes how to meet people and then start, maintain and end relationships of all kinds, both online and in the real world. Safety aspects for the real world and cyber relationships are detailed to help people minimize risk in meeting new people.

Sexual activity and sexual difficulties are presented clearly so that the reader can gain an understanding of how to find out what types of sex they might like and what may cause sensory difficulties for them as individuals. Examples of how autism spectrum adults have managed to have happy sexual and asexual relationships are given along with explanations of common sexually transmitted infections and diseases and how to have a healthy sex life.

This book was written for the individuals and families who have been asking me over the past few years: how do I meet someone? Can I ever have a happy relationship? Can autistics raise children successfully? How do I online-date? What kind of sex will I like? How can I enjoy a relationship? Will my son be accepted by the gay community? Am I the only transgender autistic? Why isn't there a book for my daughter that lets her know her options for adult relationships?

I hope that this book does indeed let adults on the spectrum not only know but understand their options and empower them to make choices and engage in decisions that help them to enjoy themselves and their relationships in the short and the long term.

1

Overview of Relationships and Sexuality

As people get older they form different kinds of relationships with other people than when they were children. Some relationships are sexual and some are non-sexual. Who you want to have a sexual relationship with can be affected by your sexuality.

Sexuality is the word for the category of sexual attraction to which someone belongs. Sexuality is not fixed for all people, it can change. People often change their sexuality as they grow up. Family, peer and cultural expectations can affect how people choose to express their sexuality.

You do not need to do sexual things with people who you like to spend time with; you can have non-sexual relationships. Sometimes friends engage in sexual activity together but normally this is something that happens only with adolescents and young adults. Older adults do not usually do this.

Co-workers can be friends but in some workplaces they can be disciplined or fired for engaging in sexual activity with a co-worker. A boss is not supposed to ask his or her staff to engage in sexual activity with them, and this type of request is an abuse of power in a workplace relationship.

You do not need to learn the hidden curriculum for all kinds of sexual relationships, just those that apply to your sexual orientation (another way of saying sexuality). However, first of all you need to work out what your sexuality is and then if the person that you are attracted to is of the same or a compatible sexuality.

Many people are unsure of the difference between different types of relationships; for example, when does a co-worker become a friend and when does a friendship develop into a relationship? It can help to visualize relationships through diagrams as long as you remember that relationships can change over time.

Figure 1.1 shows how relationships can intersect, so you can be friends with family members, but you may not be. A perfect long-term sexual relationship is one where you are both sexually and emotionally close to a person with whom you are friends.

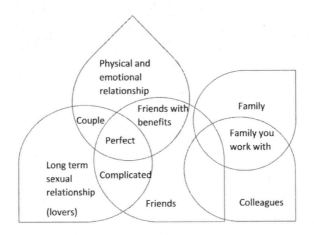

Figure 1.1 How relationships intersect

2

Gender

An additional factor involved in sexuality is how you identify your gender. For example, if you see yourself as a male this forms part of the way your sexuality is defined. Gender is not the same as your biological sex, which is the genetic determinant of your sex. Many people assume that babies are either born male or female but this is not actually true. Many babies are indeed male or female, but a number of babies are born somewhere between the two with bodies that reflect this genetic make-up. These babies are often referred to as intersex. Intersex people may not be recognized as such at birth as they may appear typical until puberty.

Intersex people can have XX, XXY or XY chromosomes, they may have typical anatomy on the outside of their body but atypical inside, or the other way round or a combination. Their appearance may seem typical until at puberty they do not develop as expected or their intersex nature may not ever be noticed. If you are intersex, you may be encouraged or even forced to live as if you were either male or female. However, more intersex people are choosing to live as intersex openly, and others are choosing to become male or female with the support of hormones and surgery. The word hermaphrodite is sometimes used to describe people who have both male and female genitalia.

Figure 2.1 The gender spectrum

It has been suggested that a larger percentage of people on the autism spectrum express themselves atypically in terms of gender and sexuality. Sadly, some people do not understand this fluidity of gender and think that everyone must be male or female. Very few countries have 'other' on official forms when asking what a person's gender is, and this has perpetuated the myth that people are always only either male or female (Figure 2.1 aims to show the variety of gender).

If you are intersex, there is no shame in this and it is not wrong or bad. It just is. How you choose to express yourself is up to you, though you may like to find support from other intersex people online or in real life. Some intersex people have found friends and family very supportive, but others feel very alone and isolated. Up to 2 per cent of babies born are intersex (Hull and Fausto-Sterling 2003), so there are lots of intersex people in the world. In some cultures there are words for a third gender, which is celebrated and honoured, whereas other cultures have a stigma attached to people who are not typically male or female identified. Being intersex does not prevent someone from having happy and fulfilling relationships.

> Kara: I have autism and I was brought up as a boy but when I was in my late teens I got sick and needed some surgery. The doctors told my family I had some aspects of a male, but I had some internal female sex organs, so I was intersex. What makes me angry is that my parents had known from my birth that there was something different about me but they never told me. I never felt male and didn't like being a boy at all. Knowing I am intersex, I have chosen to live as a female, because that is what suits me but I know some people are happy being who they are and identify as intersex. The world is changing, people know more about intersex now and more forms have male/female/other on them now.

References

Hull, C. and Fausto-Sterling, A. (2003) 'How sexually dimorphic are we? Review and synthesis.' *American Journal of Human Biology: The Official Journal of the Human Biology Council 15*, 1, 112–115.

3

Types of Sexuality

As I mentioned in the introduction, and in Chapter 2, it is important to know that, even though in school we may have learnt that there are only two genders, some people are not male (men/boys) or female (women/girls). Some people are intersex – which means that they have anatomy (body characteristics) that do not match either male or female. They may have characteristics of both, for example, a vagina and a penis. Other people are transgender; these people are born as one gender (male or female) but feel as if they have the wrong gender body. Over time many transgender (body dysmorphic) people transform their gender through the use of props (clothes, hairstyle, speech, makeup, etc.), chemicals (hormone injections) and sometimes surgery to remove unwanted body parts and create body parts that match their desired gender. This is called transitioning. Anyone of any gender can have any type of sexuality. In some countries there is a social stigma or legal discrimination against some gender types or sexual orientations (another way of describing sexuality). In other countries there is an openness and acceptance of a wide diversity of gender and sexuality.

As long as you behave in a manner that is respectful to yourself and others and legal, your gender and sexuality are nothing to be ashamed of. You do not have to be beautiful to find someone to love or be involved sexually with, nor do you have to be rich. Although films, magazines and other media imply that there is a 'standard of beauty' to which men and women should aspire, this is not true. What people perceive as beautiful is individual; for example, it may be that you see symmetry as beautiful, another person may not. Some people find age lines/wrinkles beautiful as they can be seen as illustrating the life story of that person, while other people find smooth skin youthful and they may equate youthful with beautiful.

In reality most people are attracted to a combination of personality and appearance. If you behave in a way that shows your innate kindness, are respectful and considerate to others, you will find someone who likes you for who you are, whether in real life or online. When you do, you need to ensure that mutual consent informs what you do and when.

Heterosexuality

Heterosexuality is the sexual attraction between members of the 'opposite' sex. This means that a man is sexually attracted to a woman or a woman is attracted to a man. These men and women can be transgender or not. One of the most common terms for being heterosexual is 'straight', so a man might say they are a straight man. However, many heterosexual people assume everyone is heterosexual and therefore do not feel the need to explain their sexual orientation.

When two people who are in a heterosexual relationship agree not to have sexual relationships with other people, this is known as a monogamous relationship. However, sometimes even when both people have agreed to be faithful, which means not to be sexually involved with anyone else, one or both people do have other relationships. In this case, it is referred to as being unfaithful or having an affair. A woman having a sexual relationship with a married man is often called his mistress. In some cultures having/being a mistress is widely accepted, whereas in other cultures it is viewed negatively.

Many people are not open or honest with their partner about their sexual fidelity and do not disclose what they are doing or have done. How this affects you or your partner is very personal and there is no right way of handling this situation. Having an affair is often seen as disrespectful to your partner and can hurt your partner's feelings and cause them to lose trust in you.

Heterosexuals can also have open relationships, which means that both partners are open to having other sexual relationships while they are in their main relationship. Yet other heterosexuals are in polyamorous relationships (where there are more than two people in the relationships). Most polygamous families consist of one heterosexual male who is married to two or more heterosexual females who share looking after the man and any resultant children. This is illegal in many countries and normal in some cultures.

Some people do not have sexual feelings or have experienced them so rarely that they are not sure how to identify sexual attraction. Chapter 5 will help you to understand more about sexual attraction and what it can feel like, look like and even sound like.

Homosexuality

This is the sexual attraction between members of the same sex. These men and women can be transgender or not. There are different words for men attracted to men; for example, gay, poof, fag or queer. Women who are sexually attracted to other women are referred to as lesbians, lezzies, queers or dykes. Many of the words to describe homosexual men or women are used as insults in school. This is less common in the workplace, but in some cultures or countries there are social or legal difficulties associated with being lesbian or gay. However, in other countries it is perfectly acceptable and there is legislation to prevent discrimination in the workplace, in health care or housing.

> Lynne: I always liked spending time with boys at school but then in my teens I found I wanted to spend much more time with other girls and I wanted to be really close to them. Other girls at school called me a lesbian, which I knew they meant as an insult because they shouted it and then walked away. I said I wasn't but then a girl that I became sexually involved with told me that what I was doing with her meant I was a lesbian. I thought that was amazing, this wonderful thing I was doing was called this horrid name! I decided I would call myself a dyke instead of a lesbian because it sounded strong and good. I just knew that my body and I felt more comfortable in sexual situations that were with another female. I didn't like penises and I have never found men beautiful. I guess that is how my not being sexually attracted to men showed, I didn't find them beautiful ever, and sex with them was weird: I couldn't work out what to do or why!

Many lesbian relationships are very intense when they start, and there is a widely known joke that asks what do lesbians bring to their third date? The answer is a moving truck, because, although it is not true that lesbian start living together the third time that they meet, they do tend to move into one home much quicker than other types of people. Many lesbians claim that they cannot enjoy sexual activities unless they are in love and express a preference for a long-term monogamous relationship.

However, there is another well-known joke that refers to lesbian years as dog years (i.e. one year in a lesbian relationship is like seven years in any other type of relationship). Perhaps due to the intensity of emotions in most lesbian relationships, they do not often last forever. However, they can, and many lesbian families raise children together and go on to live together happily even when the children have left home.

Other lesbians are open about their enjoyment of sexual activities and they are happy to engage in this with women they have just met, 'friends with benefits' and other casual relationships as well as in longer term committed relationships.

Gay men are just as varied in the types of relationships in which they engage, from lots of quick sex with strangers to long-term committed monogamous relationships. Gay men can appear to be more willing to have open relationships, where they live with their long-term committed partner and have sex with other people whenever they want, but never in their own home. Each relationship is different and it is important to discuss the boundaries of what is and is not acceptable for you both in your relationship.

Some lesbians and gay men choose to have children together and co-parent in a variety of different ways. This has happened for a long time and research has been done in a number of countries over a number of years that consistently shows that children of lesbian and/or gay parents are as well-adjusted as other children and do not suffer or become damaged because of their non-traditional family structure.

Bisexuality

This the sexual attraction to both the opposite and same sex, such as man to man and to woman, woman to woman and to man. These men and women can be transgender or not. Some people do not believe bisexuality is real and can say things like, 'they just want to have their cake and eat it'. This phrase does not mean anything about cake, instead it means they want to be able to have sexual relationships with both men and women. Some people seem to resent this and can be very unkind to bisexual people. Often people assume that bisexuals have more than one sexual relationship at a time, though this may or may not be the case. Heterosexuals and homosexuals can also have more than one sexual relationship at a time.

> Lynne: I thought everyone was bisexual, because I was attracted to women and I couldn't imagine anyone else not being, but I saw my female friends and peers from university and work being attracted to and having relationships with men, so I assumed everyone was attracted to both and therefore bisexual. Because I thought this, I tried having a relationship with a couple of men (one after the other, not at the same time), just in case not liking the first relationship was just a one off. However, what I realized was that I just didn't enjoy being sexually involved with men, I like them as friends but I just find their bodies so unattractive. In contrast, I am very comfortable with my body and my partner's body if my partner is female. It just feels more natural to me. The men that I knew were bisexual and seemed to be genuinely attracted to both men and women and talked to me about the way that they were attracted to people and the gender was irrelevant for them.

Some people are genuinely bisexual, while others may actually be homosexual but for personal/social/cultural reasons they are in heterosexual marriages and choose not to accept or use the term homosexual to describe themselves. This may be because of family, cultural, religious and/or social pressures or due to not knowing that there was any option to be true to who they are and how that could be possible.

Bisexual people can be in any kind of relationship: married, monogamous, polygamous, open, etc. Again this is very much up to the individual people involved in the relationship and should be discussed openly and clearly whenever necessary.

Asexuality

This is the lack of sexual attraction and sexual interest towards/ in other people. People who are asexual can be single (not in a sexual or intimate relationship), or they can be in an intimate relationship where there is little or no sexual activity, or they can be in a sexual relationship. Often asexual people who are in sexual relationships say that they would prefer not to be sexual but they are afraid of upsetting their partner/spouse or feel pressured into being sexual. Some people on the autistm spectrum prefer to be non-sexual because of their personal sensory issues. However, for other people on the autism spectrum sexual activity can be very pleasurable. Some asexual people report that others are not very understanding and can't believe that people choose not to be sexually active. An unkind word that others can say about people who do not respond to sexual requests is frigid. Some people identify as gay/lesbian asexuals and these people would prefer to be in a same-sex relationship with no sexual activity.

> Claire: I just don't like to be touched sexually, I'd rather I never had to be in those situations. I find the whole thing sensorially really overwhelming.

> People are quite shocked that I am happy being asexual, they think that maybe I just can't find the right partner but I like my life without sexual relationships.

Some adults on the autism spectrum who are asexual talk about a preference for objects over people, and their asexuality is a natural extension of this. There is nothing wrong with being asexual, although many young people say that they find it hard to be accepted when they tell people they are asexual. Part of the reason for this is that many cultures have become highly sexualized, where, for example, adverts commonly use sexual imagery. There are online support groups and a growing awareness and understanding of asexuality.

Polysexuality

This is the sexual attraction to more than one gender, but it is the word often chosen by people who either choose not to identify with a particular gender or who do not want to be known as bisexual because bisexual implies only two genders: male or female. Intersex people or their sexual partners may choose to call themselves polysexual. This is not a common word as people who were intersex used to be made to live as either a girl or a boy when they were children and felt as if they had to look like a man or a woman as an adult. In many parts of the USA, Canada, Europe, Australia and New Zealand, children are allowed to be intersex and to choose to live in a way that suits them. For example, many official forms have now been changed from male/female to male/female/other.

Pansexuality/omnisexuality

This is the sexual attraction towards people as individuals rather than to people because of their gender. Some pansexuals describe themselves as gender blind, as to them gender is not relevant in determining whether they will be sexually attracted to others. Adults on the autism spectrum are often attracted to specific people rather than to complete genders; however, they may or may not define themselves as omnisexual.

Transsexual

Transsexual is not a sexuality, rather it is where a person changes their body to move from appearing as one sex to another. This is similar but not the same as being transgender, which is where a person identifies with a different gender to their birth gender. In both cases the person can be heterosexual, homosexual, asexual, polysexual or pansexual.

Sue: I was born male. My chromosomes say that I am male. But my gender identity is female. I was told by my therapist during my transition that there are 13 different aspects that contribute to a person being considered male or female. At the core is gender identity, a deeply ingrained feeling that someone is male or female (or in between), and that that identity is almost always recognizable early, as early as 18 months.

I suspect that gender identity for someone who is on the autism spectrum is different to gender identity for a neurotypical. While I knew early on that I wasn't male, my body was male and that was that. So expression of my core identity is probably modified by aspie pragmatism. As well, I was born in the 1950s, a time when difference was frowned on. Bigotry was normal, being gay was illegal, and my father was an abusive man. It was not an upbringing that was conducive for telling anyone that I was not a boy.

The need to hide is a common feeling for anyone who is different from societal norms. This is especially true for gender dysmorphic people, and such stories have been told commonly. I am not unique. So starting from that background, how does it feel to be trans and aspie? How does anything feel when you are different? You are the one who stands out, but is not sure why. You are the one who doesn't fit in with the boy groups, nor the girl groups. You want to dress as a girl, you want to play with dolls even though you have no idea what to do with them, and you know that it is wrong somehow. You study, you watch, you try to understand, you form theories of the world and of people, then you go back to watching, and modelling. And then you learn to escape into your books and fantasy, rereading the same books multiple times because they are the same each time and understandable. You read books about girls until you are discovered and ridiculed, so you turn to fantasy, dragons and unicorns, and science fiction, and find this is acceptable because boys read that too. So it's weird, but gender safe.

At seven years I knew that I was going to be a girl when I grew up. I had no idea why I wasn't, but I knew that it was wrong somehow. Again, the aspie pragmatism: life continues. Sex change wasn't discussed in my house, and I never thought to ask, never even considered that such things were possible. Cross-dressing is a path that most trans people take. Not as a sexual fantasy, but somehow it is comfortable.

I have one body, I was born with it, so it can't be wrong. But I knew I wasn't a real male. Like many other trans, I learned to hide that, even from myself. When I started the trip towards transition, it was initially done quietly, then publicly. I visited a gender counsellor after searching through an early version of the internet (in 1995). The counsellor gave me books to read, in particular *True Selves* by Chloe Ann Roundsly, and I found that I wasn't the only trans person in the world, and that many of the others had a similar story. Not only that, but sex change was possible and had been done for years, even in New Zealand.

I joined a cross-dressing group where the organizers held 'training' evenings on deportment, dress sense, and makeup. It's funny to look back on that stage when I was convinced that gender was binary, and I had to do my best to pass as a woman. Another aspect that is more aspie, is the decision that I would stay as the kids' father. They still call me 'dad' to the immense confusion of their friends.

No two trans are the same. Typically most transsexuals are open about themselves during transition but end up keeping things private again later. Somehow, non-transsexuals get caught up in the physical aspects and ask rude questions: have you had surgery? etc. Whereas the change is really about acceptance of one's self. It is not polite to ask what someone's status is: post-op, pre-op, whatever. And now there is more awareness of gender fluidity, people ask few questions anyway. I know that my sister-in-law can't conceive of someone being neither male nor female but somewhere inbetween. For most transsexuals, there is the standard binary gender. But for me, probably the aspie side, I know that genetically I'm not female, so I find it more comfortable to see myself more female than male, while retaining some aspects of both. It is that pragmatism again.

I met other trans people in Wellington by joining a group in order to find out how to do the transition thing. I joined a group in Christchurch, and became good friends with a couple who have since been married. But I never think about going with someone. I was chased by a lesbian woman in Christchurch who wanted to date, and got so frightened by my lack of awareness in how to proceed that I refused to answer my phone to her, and I still wouldn't have a clue. I've only ever had one partner in my life, and am not looking for anything new. Less than 10 per cent of transsexuals ever go back to having a sexual partner apparently, so I knew what I was getting into when I walked out on my marriage. And, like many aspies, I am more comfortable being alone.

4

Types of Relationships

Co-worker or colleague

This is someone you work with (in near proximity to or in the same building). If someone describes you as their co-worker, they mean that they do not have a close relationship with you and interactions should be less intimate than with your friends. This means that you share less personal information with them than you would with a friend. You can ask co-workers for help with work tasks or things at work and they should help you. In turn you should help them when they ask for help. If a co-worker or colleague asks you to do their work for them more than two or three times, this person is being unkind. They are taking advantage of you and it is OK when they ask you again to say, 'Sorry I can't help today as I have a lot of work to do myself.' You can say this whenever you want, but you must then appear to be busy with your work.

Even though this is a contradiction to the above, many people meet their partners or future wives/husbands at work. If you are sexually attracted to someone at work, that is OK but you must be aware of the rules in your workplace about relationships between people at work. Being open and honest is important if you are having a workplace romance/ relationship. If your workplace partner is your boss and they want to hide the relationship, this may indicate a number of possible problems that you should be aware of:

▶ It may be expressly forbidden for superiors to have sexual/intimate relationships with their juniors, as is the case in the military, for example.

▶ The relationship may be 'a bit of fun' for your boss and they have no intention of it becoming long-term or committed.

▶ Your boss is worried that the relationship may cause people to gossip about you/them/the relationship.

▶ Your boss may already be in another relationship.

Workplace interactions can be very easy or very difficult, and this is the case for all people, not just those of us on the autism spectrum. There is a great poster from www.phdcomics.com (Cham 2013) that is a guide to relationships between employees in universities and other academic institutions. Although this guide is very simplistic and meant to be humorous, there is sadly some truth in this as many people new to academia will experience. The guide suggests that people who work in the following relationships view each other in the following ways:

Table 4.1 Guide to relationships between employees in universities

Working relationship	Way the people view each other
Different departments and different subject areas	Who cares (no interest in each other)
Same department and different subject area	Colleague (will work together in a civil manner)
Different departments but same subject area	Collaborator (will work together on an equal basis)
Same general subject but different specialism	Conference buddy – happy to coauthor academic papers and present at conferences together
Same department and same subject area	Bitter enemy – these people may be nice to you in your presence, but will sabotage your work and talk negatively about you to others whenever you are not around

Adapted from Cham 2013

It can be very confusing to those of us on the spectrum when people are unkind at work; however, it can help to know what non-autistic people say about these kinds of negative relationships: people at work can be unkind to new colleagues because they feel that their job or their status is threatened. It might be that the new person has more qualifications and/ or experience than them and this makes them feel insecure, which often results in being unkind or trying to make the new person look useless to others.

People can also be unkind because the new person has broken some unwritten rules about the social structures in the workplace. Most workplaces have a hierarchy of power and non-autistic people are very aware of this and of where they are in that hierarchy. Many people on the autism spectrum do not see this or show no interest in traditional forms of power. This can annoy or upset others, who can react quite unprofessionally and with behaviour that is contradictory – nice in person and awful about the person when they are not present.

Even being good at your job can cause some non-autistic people to be unkind in the workplace. This is because they think that you being good at your job makes them look bad and, instead of wanting to improve themselves, they are just concerned with stopping you from appearing to be more skilled/knowledgeable than them. This can be particularly distressing for people on the autism spectrum, who tend to want to do their best all the time and cannot see the logic in this viewpoint.

Bullying is endemic in many workplaces around the world, with research indicating that bullying causes loss of productivity, stress, distress and high staff turnover. It is never OK to belittle people, their appearance or their work, and if this happens to you, you have choices about what to do. You can choose to ask the person to clarify exactly what they mean – perhaps they are trying to provide some constructive feedback but do not have very good communication skills – or you can choose to ignore it or report it. All three choices have implications and may affect your career in that workplace. Many people choose instead to look for another job and leave as soon as possible.

People on the spectrum can be misunderstood by their co-workers/colleagues and this can also cause problems, including them thinking that you are bullying them. If you have constructive feedback for someone who you work with, it is better to talk to them by themselves first in a calm, quiet voice. You have to be specific about what they could improve and how, as well as specifying something that they do well. Ending workplace conversations on a positive note can ensure that you do not damage workplace relationships.

However, the social nature of the non-autistic world means that these hierarchies and unwritten rules about who must do things on time versus who does not get into trouble for doing things late are real and understood by most typical employees and their employers. This is the area that causes most difficulty for those on the autism spectrum who have jobs, in trying to keep their jobs while minimizing stress and anxiety. It is really hard for people on the spectrum to understand the unwritten rules and hierarchies, and hard for them to work out who they can relax and be themselves around, and who they need to be more formal with. It is OK to be a little quiet and reserved, but polite, until you are more confident about how to interact with your new colleagues. Saying that you are shy initially is a useful and socially acceptable thing to say when you start at a new workplace.

Another issue that can cause problems in workplace relationships is where colleagues and/or bosses are aware of your autism spectrum diagnosis but do not understand it properly. This can result in people treating you as if you are stupid, even if you have more qualifications or experience than they do. For example, they may talk slowly and/or loudly to you. This may be because of ignorance rather than prejudice, but it can be hard to tell the difference. If you have some accommodations at work to enable you to perform your job as effectively as possible, these can also be misunderstood or resented by some people.

If you would like to have some modifications to your work area or the way you work, but have not yet asked for them out of fear/anxiety about how your colleagues and co-workers will respond, you can do this using strategies discussed by Stephen Shore over the past few years. He suggests that you ask in such a way that talks about what you need specifically, and exactly why it would help, rather than saying that you need something because of your autism/Asperger's. For example, you might ask your boss if you could have a desk lamp instead of sitting under the fluorescent light. You could explain that the fluorescent light gives you headaches, which mean that you need to take a break every hour, whereas if you had a desk lamp instead, you could work more productively for your whole shift/day. When talking to co-workers about why you have a lamp and your desk is off to the side so that it is not directly under the fluorescent light, you could say that you negotiated this as you found that the lights were giving you headaches.

Although this might be directly as a result of your sensory sensitivities, it is easier for non-autistic people to accept and understand the specific changes and reasons than to discuss it in terms of your autism spectrum diagnosis and what it means for you. This sort of explanation can promote positive relationships with your colleagues and managers, whereas demanding changes can lead to resentment and negative interpersonal relationships.

Another issue that is common for autism spectrum adults in the workplace is around socializing. Many autism spectrum adults go to work to do their work and that is all they want to do during working hours. However, for non-autistic people, workplaces are also social environments and smoke/cigarette and coffee breaks are times to have a chat with others who they like or would like to get to know more. This can distract people from their work, but can be prioritized by some people. Consequences depend on the workplace and on the individuals concerned and this can further confuse autism spectrum employees.

If you are a manager and on the autism spectrum, it is important to understand that non-autistic people are social and require time to interact socially, just as autism spectrum adults require time to focus on the details of their work.

If you hear people at work talking about other people at work, it is a good idea to listen to what they are saying and how they are saying it for a few days before making any decisions whether to join in or not. You should be listening to their tone of voice and the words they are using: are these kind, caring, compassionate, cruel, angry, neutral (or any other type of emotion)? If the people are mainly being unkind or negative about other co-workers, it can be tempting to join in their conversations by saying mean things too. This, however, will not make these people your friends and it could lead to complications at work that will impact on you. For example, if the person you were mean about is actually friends with one of the group but you hadn't realized this, then the whole group may start to dislike you. To avoid this you could read a book or listen to music at break times and just smile or nod at people.

If the people are generally having a pleasant break, you may want to join in their conversations. It is important to realize that co-workers may not want to hear you talk about things that you find interesting. Instead you will need to talk with them about the things that they are already talking about. Sometimes you will find a colleague who shares your interests and, if this is the case, you may be able to chat away on that topic happily all break for weeks or even months.

A brief overview of work events is useful here as sometimes people can assume that the office/workplace relationship structure is different at a work event, especially if alcohol or travel are involved. However, this is not actually the case, it is still not OK to tell your boss that you think they could do their job more effectively, even if they and/or you have had a lot of alcohol to drink. Many people have got fired/sacked/made redundant after behaving in an unacceptable manner at a work event. Unacceptable behaviour includes: touching or trying to kiss someone, making personal comments about someone's body or sexuality, photocopying you own body parts, being aggressive and/or violent. If you do not drink alcohol and find that alcohol is an integral part of work events, it is OK to say that you need to leave early and then leave after half an hour or so.

If you are at a conference for work, the conference dinner may be seen as a time for getting to know your colleagues/boss better; however, it is important to understand that the meal will not be served for some hours after the event starts. At such events, wine and/or beer are often free and some people can drink a lot of alcohol in these situations, as they take it as an opportunity to get drunk. If you do not drink alcohol it is fine to drink something else. If you do drink alcohol, ensure that you drink slowly or stop after a few drinks, to ensure you do not say or do anything that can have negative consequences for you. You will be expected to stay until the meal is over if you attend this function, and this can take a long time during which you will be expected to talk not just to the person/s that you know from work but also to the other people at your shared table.

Simple topics that are usually safe are around work, asking the other people what they do/who they work with/for and where they are from. It is not advisable to start a sexual relationship or engage in sexual activities with anyone who is not your partner at a work event or conference. If you notice your colleagues and/or manager doing this, it could make you think that it is OK or it could make you feel very uncomfortable. It is easier to go to bed early, claiming that you feel tired from the travelling and/or getting up early that morning (even if this is not true, it is a socially acceptable reason). This avoids you having to work out what to do with information about your boss and/or colleagues that you would rather not have!

Finally, each workplace will have some unwritten rules around celebrations. This will be known to most people who work there and not always obvious to you or new staff. For example, in some workplaces, birthdays are celebrated, while in others they are not. In the places they are celebrated, either the person whose birthday it is, is meant to provide a cake and or some snacks, or the rest of the staff do this. It is up to you whether or not to let your co-workers know when your birthday is. However, if you do and it occurs over a weekend, you will still be expected to celebrate it on either the Friday before or the Monday after!

Where workplaces celebrate religious events, such as Diwali or Christmas, it is often optional to join in with present giving or other social events. It is OK to say no to these but, if you do want to join in, the rules are often quite explicit; for example, buy a gift that costs less than $5. Secret Santa is where you are allocated a person to buy a gift for and they are not told who bought the gift. If you do this and are allocated someone you do not like or know, it is not OK to then decide not to participate. Just buy a gift that is neutral, such as candles or festive decorations.

To improve your relationships with co-workers, smile when you see them first each day and say hi. You do not need to do this more than once in the day. However, looking up from your work and turning your head towards them while smiling if they interrupt your work will help others to decide that you are nice. Shouting should always be avoided in the workplace unless you are a sports coach, or the noise where you work is such that you have to shout to be heard. If you have a naturally loud voice, try to be aware that others can perceive this as aggressive.

If you are in a workplace that has a kitchen, it can be really appreciated by your colleagues if you offer to make them a cup of tea/coffee/hot chocolate every now and then. This is particularly supportive if you offer when you know a colleague has just received some bad news or if you think that they are feeling tired or unwell. You do not need to do this all time unless it is part of your job to do so. Signs that someone is unwell are things like being much quieter than usual, skin tone is paler or they look feverish.

Friends

Sometimes we really like someone we work with. We can make friends with people we work with or people we meet at college, university or any other place. People usually spend some time together with their friends but this time together can be online or in real life. Sometimes friends share an apartment or house and then the people are called flatmates. Mate is another word for friend and, in this context, flat is another word for apartment, even though it could be a condo or a house.

Friends and flatmates are some of the relationships that can develop into sexual relationships over time. It is useful to spend time getting to know someone as their friend before becoming involved with them sexually and/or romantically as this will help you to understand if you do want to spend time with them or not and, if so, in what sort of relationship. It will also give them time to understand you and your interests.

It is important to know that if you become sexually/romantically involved with a friend, and then things go wrong and you end your sexual relationship (known as breaking up), then they may not want to be your friend anymore. Some friendships work very well as sexual relationships too but others do not. It is often said that you can find someone to have sex with far more easily than you can find a good friend, and this is worth thinking about. One of the phrases that is used to suggest it is easy to get a new partner is 'there are plenty more fish in the sea', which means that the world is very large with lots of people who may be compatible with your sexuality and personality.

Non-autistic people have particular expectations around behaviour of, and interactions with, people that they call friends. These expectations seem to be culturally based and so are not the same for everyone. For people on the autism spectrum we think of people as friends who we feel comfortable around and who like us and with whom we can interact without constantly worrying about whether we have done or said something wrong. We may only see our friends occasionally in real life or rarely talk to them on the phone and this is perfectly acceptable. On the other hand, we may talk to our friends daily or Skype with them frequently. However, there do not seem to be any expectations within the autistic community around how often friends should contact each other.

Non-autistic expectations of friendship can include type of interaction (phone/in person, etc.), frequency (daily/ weekly/monthly) and emotional connection. For example, non-autistic friends may meet up and chat/gossip or go out drinking together on a regular basis, at least once a week. For most people on the autism spectrum, this would not be fun and it is unlikely that they would want to do this. Non-autistic parties have unwritten social rules about when to arrive, leave and how to behave in order to demonstrate friendship and respect. These can be complicated and impact on the way people perceive each other.

Expected party behaviour

Different types of parties require different behaviour; for dinner parties or events involving sit down meals, it is important to arrive within five to ten minutes of the start time on the invitation, *unless* the invitation says, for example, 6.30 for 7pm, in which case you need to arrive by 7pm as this is when the meal starts. For parties without sit down meals it is OK to arrive 30–60 minutes late unless the host prefers punctuality (they could be from a culture where being on time is very important, or they or their family members are on the autism spectrum). If you need to arrive later, it is polite to text/message or phone to ask if it is OK if you come at X time as you are 'busy before but would really like to come'.

It is polite to take a small gift or drink with you when you go to a party, which you should give to the host on your arrival. However, for college/university student parties this is not the same. In these cases, you should bring your own drink (but still be willing to share it) and put it with all the other drinks, usually in the kitchen or on a big table or space on the floor. You can take alcoholic or non-alcoholic drinks. If you do not want to share your own drink, it is ok to take a second drink that you keep hold of. If you take beer, it is more appropriate to take a six-pack or more to share, with wine, spirits, juice or fizzy drinks one bottle is fine.

It is viewed as impolite to leave a birthday party before the cake is cut (by the person whose birthday it is). At a party with a sit down meal, it is seen as rude to leave before dessert has been served *and* finished. This is the case for conference meals and work events too. You should always try to find the host/hostess of the party and thank them and say goodbye just before you leave.

Whereas it is perfectly acceptable to leave an autism spectrum party by saying that you are tired and / or overwhelmed and so need to leave, this is not socially acceptable for most other contexts. In other contexts, it is necessary to have been at the party for at least two hours and you need to provide a socially acceptable reason to leave, which prevents people from (a) thinking you are rude; (b) thinking you are weird. It is important to note that socially acceptable excuses in this context are not necessarily true, instead they are a symbolic set of words that translate in a social context to: I like you and / or respect you and I have enjoyed my time at your party, but now I need to leave and want to leave in a polite and respectful manner. However, saying that would *not* be OK…

Things you can say when leaving a party (do not use the ones with an asterisk if you do not have that type of family life at home):

▶ Thanks for the great evening, I'm sorry I need to leave now because the babysitter has to go at [insert time that is no more than 45 minutes from the time you are saying this].*

▶ Thank you for the invite, I've had a lovely time, but I've got to go now as I've just got a new puppy that I am worried about leaving alone much longer.*

▶ I had a lovely time, thanks. I wish I could stay longer but I have to get up really early for work tomorrow so I need to get going.

▶ Thanks for having me, it was lovely. Bye.

▶ Thank you, great party, sorry I need to leave now.

Also, depending on the predominant culture represented at the party (gay/lesbian/straight/Middle Eastern/European, etc.) the host or hostess may expect a kiss on the cheek and/or a hug or nothing when you are leaving. This can be hugely confusing if you do not belong to the predominant culture. Some ways to avoid the kissing/hugging are to be holding a large bag/coat in front of you with two hands or holding your hand out as if you are going to shake his or her hand, which is what will then happen.

If you receive an invitation to a party that says RSVP, you should reply within a few days to let the person know whether or not you will be attending. Some invitations may be addressed to you and say your name +1 or plus one. This does not mean that you have to take someone with you, but it means that you can. If there is an RSVP, you should also let the host or hostess know if you are going to be bringing someone with you or not. You do not need to let them know who you are bringing straight away, so if you are not sure yet, that is OK.

If you are invited to a lot of parties/events through work or where you are studying or through family, it does not mean that you have to attend. It is OK to say, 'thanks for the invite but I can't make it'. If you text/message or email this, that is fine too. Some people on the autism spectrum find this really difficult as they feel obliged to attend unless they are actually doing something else at that time. However, 'I can't make it' can be interpreted as you being 'too busy' by the person to whom you are responding, but you may mean that you do not have the emotional energy or desire to attend. It can be very difficult for people to understand that most people on the autism spectrum expend energy being social because socializing energizes most neurotypical people.

If you are open about your autism/Asperger's, you may choose to let people know that, although you do like them, socializing can be exhausting for you. It may be that you ask friends to watch a movie or play online games or board games or have a meal with you instead of going to a bar or nightclub. This is not to say that people on the autism spectrum cannot go clubbing and enjoy it, it is just exhausting rather than energizing.

Who can be a friend?

Friends can be of any gender (male, female, transgender, intersex, gender queer and gender questioning). They can be older than you or younger than you. However, it can be viewed negatively if you try to make friends with children once you are an adult. This is because many societies have a problem with high levels of sexual abuse and exploitation of children, and these children are 'groomed' (prepared/lured) into these roles by adults pretending to be their friend.

Research has shown that having friends and being connected to your wider community supports good mental health and wellbeing. However, it can be very hard for people on the autism spectrum to understand if a person is being a good friend or if they are using us for their own benefit. Sometimes family members or long-term friends can tell us this, but we do not always listen or believe them. Therefore, we need to know how to work out if someone is a good person and if they can be a friend, as well as learning how to be friends with them. Being friends with a neurotypical person can be quite different to being friends with a neurodiverse person (someone on the autism spectrum and/or with attention deficit hyperactivity disorder (ADHD), and/or with mental health difficulties).

Friendships are not always forever: sometimes friends come into and then go out of your life. This is OK and does not mean that you or they did anything wrong. It may be that they moved away or became very busy or just changed in their thoughts around what is important for them at that moment in time. What people say and do are the things to pay attention to when you are trying to work out whether they are friends or not. These are some of the things that indicate a person is a good friend:

▶ You like to be with/around this person and have them around you.

▶ They do not judge you or make cruel/mean comments to you.

▶ They are respectful and/or kind to you.

▶ They like you because they like you and not because they are paid or told to like you.

▶ They will help you when you need help.

▶ You feel less stressed and/or more happy when you are around them.

▶ They are still available to talk to you or help you out even when things are very difficult for you.

▶ They are comfortable around you and you around them.

▶ They are OK with you being sad, angry, happy or any other emotion.

If you want to be a good friend to someone, you can do the things in the list above. However, there are a number of other things that you can do to show someone that you are a good friend to them. Some of these are listed below:

▶ Make sure that you listen to your friend. You can talk too but friends try to understand what is happening in each other's lives and how the other person is feeling. This means that you do not have to give advice, you just need to listen and show that you have heard them. Many autism spectrum adults do want advice from their friends: it is better to say that you want advice and not to give advice unless your friend specifically asks for it.

▶ If your friend is sad, ask them if they would like a hug, if you are OK with hugging people. If you do not like to hug, you could ask them if they would like a cup of tea or coffee. Many people find having a cup of tea or coffee made for them helps them to feel cared about. If you do not know what they want or need, it is OK to ask them if you can do anything to help.

▶ Do fun things with your friends – it might be necessary to take turns with who chooses the activity as sometimes friends do not find the same things fun. Laughter is a really positive expression and it is good to laugh with your friend, but not at them.

▶ Text, call, message, Skype or Facebook your friends at least once a week as this shows them that you care about them. If they say that they miss you, they expect you to say that you miss them too. This can be a little strange for adults on the spectrum, who often do not think about people who are not physically present. When a friend says they miss you, what they mean is that life is better when they are talking to you or when you are spending time with them. If you enjoy talking to or being with them, it is nice to say that you miss them too, or that you are really happy to be talking with/spending time with them today.

▶ People need to know that you care about them if they are your friends, but this does not mean that you should say 'I care about you'. It means that you should be kind and respectful and thoughtful. Thoughtful actions are giving someone a card (homemade, electronic or bought) for their birthday or a religious/cultural event that they celebrate. Also, if your friend is sick, it is a good idea to ask if you can do anything to help. Things they might need help with are getting their grocery shopping or cooking a meal.

▶ Be open with them about your autism/Asperger's and any other conditions you might have. Explain what this means for you and any issues that they should be aware of. If they have a medical or mental health condition, you could ask them if they need anything specific from you or not.

▶ Friends are honest with each other, *but* this can be difficult for some people at first. If you are asked 'does this top look nice on me?', if it looks awful, it is polite not to say that it looks awful but to say that you have seen them wearing nicer tops, or that the colour/fit/pattern is not as nice as their usual clothes. Having said this, I have friends who really like to ask me what I think of clothes when they are shopping as they are tired of buying clothes that the shop assistant said looked wonderful, only to realize at home that it looks terrible.

▶ Occasionally friends do things that we feel are really unsafe, or become unwell or severely stressed and we think that they need help. In these instances it is important to speak up and say what you are worried about and why. This can result in the person never speaking to you again or it can result in your friendship becoming stronger, and there is no way to predict which. However, if you do not speak up, and things deteriorate for your friend, and you have not stepped in to try to help, this is unethical.

How to tell when someone is only pretending to be your friend, or is not your friend

Sometimes when we meet people, or even with people we have known a long time, we want to be their friend and we assume that their interactions with us signal that they are our friend. Being friendly is *not* the same as being your friend. For example, the wait staff where you have a coffee every day many be friendly, but they are not your friends, they are just doing their job. If you have carers, or live in supported accommodation, these staff may also be friendly, but again they are just doing their jobs and are not your friends. Friends spend real or online time together outside of the workplace (theirs and/or yours) and see each other as equals in the friendship.

When people are unkind or rude and say mean things to you or to other people about you, they are not your friends. When people isolate you and purposely ignore or exclude you, they are not your friends. It is OK not to be friends with someone, but it is never OK to treat people badly, whether this is with words or actions.

Actions that demonstrate that someone is pretending to be your friend are things like:

▶ Always inviting themselves to your house at meal times.

▶ Getting you to pay for things when you are out together and never offering to pay for anything.

▶ Getting you to help plan for and organize an event like a birthday party and then not inviting you. A true friend would invite you and let you know that they will not be offended if you choose not to come because it might be overwhelming for you.

▶ Borrowing money from you and never paying it back.

▶ Being nice to you when you are alone and ignoring you or not being nice to you when other people are around.

▶ Treating you badly by being demeaning and belittling.

▶ Hitting, slapping, punching or hurting you in any way. This person does *not* like you or love you, even if they apologize and say that they will never do this again. It does not matter who this person is, if someone behaves like this to you, you must remove yourself from the situation as quietly and calmly as possible and seek medical attention to check there is no internal bleeding or broken bones, etc. Do not let the person stay with you when you speak to the doctor and / or nurses, and, if they do not want to leave, ask the medical staff to make them leave. If you are not able to speak because you are non-verbal or because you are too distressed, try to write/ type a note or draw a picture of what has happened.

If you know that your friend is being abused physically or emotionally by their partner, then you should try to talk to your friend by themselves and suggest ways that they can access help, such as a refuge or helpline.

Lucy: I thought that Debbie was my friend: we were friends all though school and she said I could be one of the bridesmaids at her wedding. We stayed friends when she was at university but didn't see each other very often as we lived in different areas. She came back to our home town when she graduated and her wedding was going to be local to me. I did get an invite, but I wasn't asked to be a bridesmaid. She told me that it was only family, but when I got there it was obvious this was a lie. I felt really sad because I knew this meant she wasn't really friends with me anymore. I don't think we have ever had contact since.

Mike: Phil said he was my friend; he used to bring his mates over to my house every Friday night, because I had my own flat. They brought lots of beer and would get so drunk that they would say they had to stay over. It ended up that they were there all weekend every weekend and I didn't even know some of the people that would come over. When I asked Phil if they could go somewhere else he got really angry and said that I was such a weirdo, I would never make any other friends if I didn't let them come over. I had to change the locks because he had a spare key and wouldn't give it back. It was awful, but when I look back I can see he wasn't my friend, he was just using me to have a nice space to hang out in and get drunk. I didn't realize adults could be as cruel as kids at school, but they can, it is just harder to work it out sometimes.

Dr Henry Cloud and Dr John Townsend have written a number of books that are summarized online on multiple sites. They also have free video advice (Cloud-Townsend Resources n.d.) that could be very useful in helping you to understand the possible explanations for the behaviour of other people. It is important to note that these writers write from a position of their Christian faith, and you may or may not want to follow their advice if you have a different moral or ethical framework. One of their core concepts is around safe (good/kind) and unsafe (bad/unkind) people and how to tell the difference between these. A summary of this concept is useful for people on the autism spectrum as we are not always able to tell the difference without explicit knowledge of what to look for.

Table 4.2 is loosely based on their ideas but simplified and clarified.

Table 4.2 Safe and unsafe people

Behaviours and attitudes of safe people (people who would make good friends or people to have relationships with)	Behaviours and attitudes of unsafe people (people who it is not advisable to be in a relationship or friends with)
Value love and interpersonal connections or positive connections to animals and/or things	May apologize but do not change their behaviour
Take responsibility for their own behaviour and sometimes blame themselves when things go wrong	Think they are perfect all the time and all problems are the fault of other people
Look for solutions to their problems instead of blaming others	Moan about their problems instead of trying to find solutions
Value trust and honesty and behave in ways that show they are trustworthy	Demand trust, even when acting in ways that demonstrate they are not trustworthy (such as lying, stealing, cheating, gossiping)
Try to learn from life and treat others well	See life as a race to the top and can treat others badly to get ahead

Boyfriend/girlfriend

When people start to date or go out with each other they often use the words boyfriend or girlfriend to describe the other person. To date means to meet up with another person and spend time with them with the intent of the relationship becoming sexual in the future. However, people who say they are going out often do not go anywhere, but spend time at each other's houses or at places they were going to anyway.

These relationships usually start out as non-sexual and may or may not become sexual. If they do become sexual, it is important that both people are old enough to be involved in sexual activity. If one of the people is not old enough (underage), the other person is committing a serious legal offence (breaking the law). Most women assume that their boyfriend or girlfriend will not be engaging in sexual activity with another person while they are their boyfriend or girlfriend. However, many men do not assume this and, if the two people do not talk about it, then the relationship can be very difficult. When two people are in a sexual relationship only with each other that is known as being monogamous or being faithful. If one or both of them are having sexual relationships with another person/ people as well, that is known as being polygamous. If people are open and honest about their polygamy this is known as an open relationship. If they are not and do not tell the people about the other(s) then they are often described as being unfaithful.

People involved in relationships are not always honest about their sexual activities or their emotions. There are lots of unspoken rules about these relationships – they are in the following chapters.

In countries where the term boyfriend is used to mean a friend who is male in addition to being used to mean a male with whom the speaker is in an emotional and sexual relationship, it can be confusing. Some people choose to use the word partner to describe the person with whom they are in an ongoing sexual relationship.

The legal age of consent (age at which a person can engage in sexual activities) varies between countries and in some places by state too. For example, in Australia the age of consent is different in different states. The age of consent can also vary depending on the gender/type of sexuality, so male homosexual sexual activities may have a different age of consent to heterosexual activities. In some countries male but not female homosexuality is illegal, and in others both may be legal/illegal. This is changing and, in many countries, homosexuals can marry or have legal partnerships with a same-sex partner.

It is important that you find out the rules about the age of consent where you live and behave according to these rules. If you do not you can end up in jail and, in many countries, on the sex offenders register for the rest of your life. This is the case even if the sex was consensual and the other person initiated it.

When you engage in sexual activities these all carry some risks to your physical health, these risks are detailed in Chapter 21. However, to prevent the transmission of sexually transmitted diseases you can have what is called 'safe sex', which means using protective barriers between your genitals/body parts and the other person's genitals/body parts. Naked skin touching naked skin is not the cause of a sexually transmitted disease, rather it is open wounds/genitalia/mouths coming into contact with the bodily fluids of the other person. Bodily fluids are things like semen, vaginal secretions, mucus and blood. Many of the fungal/viral/bacterial infections of genitals can be easily transmitted to the mouth, so oral sex is not safer than penetrative sex. However, a woman cannot get pregnant from engaging in oral sex.

Protective barriers are things like condoms (both male and female versions exist) and dental dams. These are usually made of latex and some people are allergic to latex. If you are allergic to latex gloves, you are likely to be allergic to latex condoms. In this case, talk with your health care provider about what you can use to protect your sexual health. A male condom is worn over the penis and a female condom inside the vagina. Both are also used to prevent pregnancy, although if they are not used correctly during heterosexual sex, a woman can still become pregnant.

Boyfriends/girlfriends may or may not be in long-term serious relationships. These are the words that people use to describe their current partner if they are not in a legally recognized or self-identified relationship. Some people have the same boyfriend/girlfriend for many years, while others last only a few weeks or months. An indication that your boyfriend/girlfriend is serious about being in a relationship with you is if they take you to meet their parents. If you ask them to meet your parents within a few weeks of meeting them, they may think that you are getting serious too quickly and make excuses not to do this.

You may or may not live together with your boyfriend/girlfriend. This is different for each couple, although it should be something that is discussed beforehand and not something that just happens. For example, if you are going to live together, how will your finances be organized? Who will pay the rent/mortgage/bills, etc.? It is never a good idea to give all your money to your boyfriend/girlfriend, even if you live together. Instead you could have a joint account for joint expenses and then have individual savings accounts. This is especially important if you have very different attitudes to money and/or possessions.

A good relationship with a boyfriend/girlfriend is characterized by both of you enjoying the time you spend together most of the time. You should be able to have fun together easily, even without spending money or drinking alcohol. A bad relationship would be one where you have more bad times than good. For further information about understanding when you should end a relationship see Chapter 13.

Some people worry that they are having too much or not enough sex with their boyfriend/girlfriend, or that they should/should not be having sex with that person. There is no right or wrong amount of sex, although you should not have sex just because the other person wants to if it does not feel right for you. Many people lie about how much sex they are having because they want to appear to be happy and sexually attractive. If you are asexual and have a boyfriend/girlfriend, it is fine to have no sex, just as, if you and/or your boyfriend/girlfriend is highly sexual, it is fine to have sex every day, several times a day.

You may spend time with your boyfriend/girlfriend online or in real life, with others or by yourselves. Again, there is no right or wrong for this, it is about what feels right for you. If you feel that you would like to spend more time with them, it is OK to say this. If they say that they do not want to spend more time with you, you will need to decide if you want to remain their girlfriend/boyfriend or if you would prefer to break up and be single until you meet someone who wants similar time commitments from a relationship. When thinking about this, you need to also reflect on the amount and type of other commitments a person may have, such as work, caring for others, study, health issues, etc.

> Di: I met my first boyfriend when I was still at school. We went out for about six months, which meant that we would go to school discos together. I stopped being his girlfriend when he asked someone else if I was a virgin. I thought that was so disrespectful, it was nothing to do with us and if he wanted to have sex with me he should have been talking to me about it not someone else.

> Dave: I didn't get a girlfriend until I was at college; she has Asperger's too and we just really understand each other. We studied together and would also online game together. After

about eight months we decided to try living together. When we were looking for a flat our families were really surprised that we wanted separate bedrooms. We do have sex, which my mum asked about. She wanted to know why we wanted to live together if we wanted separate bedrooms. Leila and I like to sleep in different rooms because she likes it completely dark and I like to have the curtains and windows open. We couldn't understand what everyone else was talking about until mum explained that many people have sex in their bed and then go to sleep afterwards. Not us! We like to have sex and then have something to eat, because it makes us hungry.

Adam: I thought I had a girlfriend when I sat next to the same girl at the movies a few times, but really she was just a person who liked that seat and I liked the seat that was the next one along. My brother told me that you have to actually know someone to be their boyfriend, and that means interacting with them in real life or online and finding out what they are like as people. That made me kind of sad, because I liked the idea that I had had a girlfriend. So now when I am in Second Life, I try to talk to this one woman because I really like her avatar. If we get to know each other, maybe she will be my girlfriend.

Friends with benefits

Friends with benefits is a term that means friends who occasionally engage in sexual activity with each other without any wish for a long-term monogamous sexual relationship. Usually people are fairly honest and open about this arrangement. A common slang term for this is fuck buddies. For some people this is a great way to meet their sexual needs when they are finding it difficult to meet a person with whom they want to have a sexual relationship. For other people it can lead to emotional difficulties if one of the friends becomes more emotionally attached and starts to hope for a more serious sexual relationship than the other friend. If you develop very deep attachments very quickly, this may not be for you. However, if you are comfortable with short bursts of emotional/sexual intensity followed by a return to a platonic (non-sexual) relationship you may find this kind of situation useful.

If you do get involved in a friends-with-benefits relationship, it can help to have a discussion about the boundaries of that relationship. For example, if one of you meets someone else they want to start a relationship with, is the sexual part of your relationship over, or will it continue? Will the new person be told about the sexual element of your relationship or is it a secret? How often will you meet up? How will you know if you are meeting up for sex or just to hang out as friends?

An example of how to manage this is illustrated by James and Lara. James and Lara met though an online advert for a bisexual social group. When they met up in person at the group, they really liked each other and became friends. However, they were also sexually attracted to each other. Over a number of years, whenever one of them was single, they would phone the other one up every few months and ask 'Do you want to fuck?'; If the answer was yes, they would meet up at James' house and have sex. If it was no, they would chat on the phone for a bit and there were no hurt feelings. They still saw each other at the bisexual social group from time to time, but always just as friends.

> Lara: I liked James, but I didn't want to be his regular partner, I just really enjoyed sex with him. He didn't love me, we had fun when we were together and sex was always amazingly good and that was all that we were interested in. I always thought he was really respectful to me. If I said no, he was always like, oh OK no problem, take care. I could have been one of seven

women or the only one, it made no difference, he was nice and it was fun.

An example of friends with benefits going wrong is what happened with Joe and Richard. Joe and Richard had been friends for about four years. One night they left a bar together and went back to Joe's apartment. They had had a lot to drink and were both quite drunk. Both of them decided it would be a good idea to have sex, which they did. They were both fine with this and continued to meet up as friends in the next few weeks. However, Richard was falling in love with Joe and began to get jealous if Joe went home with anyone else. Richard didn't tell Joe how he was feeling and he started to get more and more jealous until he yelled at Joe when they were out in a bar one night. Joe had no idea why his friend was jealous, because in Joe's mind they were just friends with benefits. Joe decided that Richard was not really a good friend because of his behaviour and stopped seeing him completely.

> Joe: Richard and I had been friends for ages before we started to have sex sometimes, but then Richard got all possessive and weird. He wasn't my boyfriend so I don't know why he started to act as if he was. In the end it was too much hassle to stay friends.

Casual relationships

These are sexual relationships where the main or only reason the two people meet up is to engage in sexual activity. Usually people are fairly honest about this arrangement. Young adults as well as older adults can be engaged in casual relationships. Even though the people in casual relationships have no long-term commitment, there are a number of unwritten rules that guide this arrangement too – they are in the following chapters. Some people in casual relationships are not even friends with each other. This kind of relationship can also be known as a no-strings affair. Many people who want to be in this kind of relationship advertise online or through phone dating sites.

Sometimes one of the people in a casual relationship can start to develop feelings for the other person, like Richard in the above scenario. If these feelings do not go away, the relationship will either end because the other person is not interested in that type of relationship, or it may develop into a more emotional and long-term relationship. It is good to be very clear and open with someone about whether or not you are open to having an emotional/social element to a casual relationship, or if you are only interested in the person in a sexual way.

Often in casual relationships, there is very little contact between the people except to arrange when to meet to engage in sexual activity. This can be risky at the beginning of a casual relationship, as neither of the people knows the other one well and it is possible that someone is wanting to engage in sexual violence or violence rather than having a consenting casual relationship. For this reason, it is important to understand all the safety aspects of starting a sexual relationship. These are covered in Chapter 7.

An example of a casual relationship that works well is Edward and Yola. Edward and Yola are both bisexual and in long-term same-sex relationships. They met online through a dating site for people seeking affairs and both of their partners know about Edward and Yola's sexual relationship. Once a week Edward and Yola meet up after work for a drink, a chat and then they go to Yola's house as her partner works on that night. At Yola's house they chat some more and then have sex. Edward always goes home before Yola's partner arrives home from work. Edward and Yola say that they are not friends and that the relationship, although long-term, is only about sex and nothing else.

> Yola: I met Edward online, he was looking for a female for casual sex and I thought that sounded great. I love my partner very much but I miss having sex with men too, so this solves that problem for me. My partner says that I see having sex with someone the way most people see having a cup of tea with someone. I have no idea what she means, but Edward says it is about emotional attachment. He likes that I am on the spectrum, he says I am interesting and that when I say I am not interested in being emotionally involved with him he can believe it. Edward says this makes it easy and that there are no complications.

An example of a casual relationship going wrong is Aiden and Zara. Aiden and Zara met at a bar after work. They were both single and started a sexual relationship. Zara was very open about this being a no-strings affair and that she was not wanting a long-term relationship. Aiden found that when he had not seen or talked to Zara for a few days he really missed her and wanted to spend more time with her. He started to phone Zara every day, and try to set a date to see her, even if they couldn't have sex. Zara was polite but clear about the no strings, no emotional involvement. Aiden was hurt, thinking there must be something wrong with him. When he tried to talk to Zara she became annoyed, explaining again that she had been open and honest and he had agreed to the terms and conditions at the start of the relationship. Aiden did not mean to develop an emotional attachment to Zara, it had just happened, which it can do.

> Zara: I told Aiden it was no strings – this phrase is very clear, it means no emotional involvement. I just wanted to see him occasionally. For me sex seems to connect me to myself, I can't really explain it, it is maybe about being on the autism spectrum.

I don't often feel connected to myself or anyone else. When I have sex, I connect to myself, it's like I know I exist then. Aiden wanted to see me more often and to just go out for dinner and stuff. I just don't want to do that kind of thing, what would I talk about?! He doesn't know I'm autistic; he doesn't really know much about me except my email and phone number.

One night stands

This has nothing to do with standing nor often a night! It refers to a brief sexual encounter between two people who have not met before or who do not know each other very well. There is no money exchanged after this sexual encounter. If someone pays someone else for sex, this is where one of the people sells sex and someone buys. This is illegal in many countries but not others. Men who sell sex are often called rent boys and women who sell sex are called prostitutes. Selling sex is a very dangerous activity especially where it is illegal. Buying sex can be safe where it is legal and regulated but it can also be very dangerous for both the sellers and buyers.

Escort services often sell sex as well, though some are just selling companionship by the hour. In this instance the person contacts an escort company on the phone or online and pays for a man or woman to come and spend some time with them. Sometimes the escort will offer sexual activities for extra money, even in countries where this is illegal. If you take up their offer you are breaking the law in countries where it is illegal, and can be prosecuted, fined and even sent to prison. Unlike on television and in movies, escorts are not spending time with their clients because they like them or want to make friends with them, they are doing it to make money. This is also a dangerous occupation as some clients can become aggressive or even violent.

In a country where it is legal, if you pay someone for sex, you should have agreed the price and activities beforehand. Brothels are safer places to do this than public areas. You should never be violent or aggressive to a sex worker or refuse to pay them. You can be prosecuted for these acts.

One night stands usually occur in nightclubs, raves, parties with alcohol or drugs or after any of these events. If you engage in this kind of sexual activity you must ensure you use condoms and/or dental dams to protect yourself against sexually transmitted diseases and/or pregnancy. It is also important to limit what you do sexually with people you do not know or who are drunk/drugged. For example, if you like to engage in bondage activities, you should only do this with people you know well and/or who are sober. This is because the risks of becoming a victim of sexual violence are much higher when drugs and/or alcohol are involved, and if you are tied up you cannot protect yourself.

Lesbians engage in one night stands less often than all other groups (except for asexuals, who do not engage in sexual activities). Gay men are often said to have the most active sex lives, with many engaging in a number of sexual encounters in one day/night with a variety of partners. Of course this is a generalization and some gay men are in long-term monogamous relationships, and some lesbians engage in sex with women they have just met.

> Di: I have had some really good fun on a one night stand (usually for a few hours in the evening, and we were lying down), but I wish someone had told me about how emotional or vulnerable you can feel while having sex or just afterwards. Even during a one night stand I think that sex shouldn't be a frivolous act. We have asked another person to get naked and spread out all of their insecurities. There has to be respect given to a person if

they do that. No one is better than anyone else before during or after that act.

Kara: My best friend was religious and so didn't believe in sex before marriage, which was fine, but for some reason she decided that oral sex wasn't sex. I guess I wasn't very kind in the way I thought about her, but I thought that she was really silly because she could still get sexually transmitted diseases and I heard lots of guys rating her performance on 'blow jobs'. I had to look that up before I knew what they meant (stimulating a penis with a mouth) and I was stunned, she wouldn't let guys touch her genitals but she would let lots of them put theirs in her mouth! When I talked to her about why, she said it was fun and the guys liked her when she did it. It was kind of sad really because they may have liked what she was doing but I don't think they liked her – they certainly didn't respect her.

Tony: I'm a gay man and have Asperger's. I don't understand one night stands at all. I feel such an emotional connection when I have sex with someone, I don't get why I would do this just for fun like some people have a beer. Not for me.

Partner/spouse (husband or wife)

Your partner is the person with whom you are involved in a long-term committed relationship. If you marry this person they can then be called your husband or wife (spouse). Some people who have civil partnerships call their partner their wife or husband. Civil partnerships are usually for people who are the same gender as, in many countries, lesbian and gay couples cannot marry. If you have a partner or a husband/wife you should both be committed, open and honest.

Some of these relationships are not monogamous and some are. It is up to the individual people in the relationship.

However, most societies expect marriages to be monogamous, although there are also cultures and places where men can marry more than one wife at a time. Some cultures used to practice fraternal polyandry, where a woman would have multiple husbands, all of whom were brothers. However this practice has become illegal in most of those countries in the past 50 years or so.

In some cultures you can marry someone of any gender and in others you cannot. For intersex people living in some countries, the sex listed on their birth certificate will define who they can marry; for example, a male may only marry a female in some countries, so an intersex person who was called male on their birth certificate may only be allowed to legally marry a person listed as female on their birth certificate, regardless of how they identify their gender as an adult.

Generally partners/spouses live together and share a bed, though this is not the case for all people. Some couples live apart due to work commitments or because the sensory or emotional needs of one or both people involved means the relationship works better that way. People who are in long-term committed relationships may or may not be sexually intimate some or all of the time. Sometimes one person would like to have a lot more sexual intimacy than the other person and this can cause problems when they cannot agree on frequency or type of sexual intimacy. This is often referred to as sex drive incompatibility or difference. Your sex drive is the level of sexual activity that you would like, and if yours is low and your partner's sex drive is high, this can lead to relationship problems.

This kind of problem is very common and can be difficult to resolve. Sexual desire is different for different people. If someone is not experiencing sexual desire they can become disinterested in sexual intimacy and this can make the other person in the relationship feel rejected and hurt. Sometimes this can be resolved through therapy/counselling, and other times it can't. Side effects of some medications can decrease sexual desire, as can stress, tiredness, depression, anxiety and feeling unwell. In addition, people can just have completely different levels of sex drive. It can be easier for some people to engage in sexual intimacy when they are not experiencing desire than other people, so it may not be possible to just 'do it'. Again, this can lead to feelings of hurt and rejection or to feelings of inadequacy. It is important to talk about how you feel and what your sexual desires and expectations are.

If you do not like much sexual intimacy because of sensory issues, you need to be very clear about this as your partner would not want to be causing you distress instead of pleasure. Sexual activities are meant to be pleasurable for everyone who is engaging in them. If you like lots of sex because of the way it makes you feel but your partner prefers a lot less sex, this does not mean that they find you unattractive or that they don't love you. Sexual desire and love are not always related, though for some people they are. If talking about these issues does not help you or your partner to feel fully accepted and valued, you may find counselling beneficial. However, you will need to find a counsellor who understands the autism spectrum and some of the unique issues that can occur in relationships which involve autistics.

Partners/spouses often share finances as well as living accommodation. They often socialize together, although some couples do maintain their individuality through friendships and social contact with their own friends. With some couples, one person will be more responsible for taking care of the house and making meals than the other, but in other relationships these are shared equally. There is no right and wrong in this, although one person should not be doing so much that it is stressful or exhausting if the other person contributes so little that they are spending most of their time relaxing.

Non-consensual

Unfortunately some sexual encounters are not wanted by one of the people involved; these are called sexual assaults. Rape is a specific kind of sexual assault. If you do not want to engage in any kind of sexual activity with anyone you do not have to. You should say no clearly and loudly. If the person uses physical force to make you, once you are able to get away from them you should get help straight away. You may need medical assistance and may choose to report the crime against you. It does not matter what your gender is, you have the right to say no and to expect that your no is respected.

If you are with someone and kissing them, if you start to do something else, for example, removing their clothing, you must stop immediately if they say no. You must also stop as soon as they say stop or don't do that. If you do not stop, you are not only committing a crime but hurting that person. Non-consensual sex can be very emotionally confusing and distressing, and it is useful to seek counselling if you are distressed by something that has happened to you, even if it was years ago. Some people do not want to seek counselling and feel that they do not need it. That is OK too, it is up to you.

Engaging in sexual activity with people who are under the legal age of consent is a specific crime in many countries and people who do this are often called paedophiles. This has very serious legal consequences for the adult and can be very damaging for the child. Taking sexual photographs or using photographs of children under the age of consent for sexual gratification is also illegal. This comes under child pornography laws. If both of you are under the age of consent and text naked photos to each other you can still both be charged with possessing, creating and even distributing child pornography. All these charges are very serious and can result in life-long consequences, such as inclusion on a sex offenders register.

If you have consensual sex but a video recording or still photos are taken of this, both partners have to consent to the use of these pictures/videos in any public format. Texting or electronic sharing of these with your sexual partner or anyone else is not advised as they can be forwarded or posted publically at any time in the future, which can be both upsetting and have other negative consequences. If the sex recorded was non-consensual, the video or photographic evidence can be used by the police and the court in any prosecution or criminal charges.

If you are married or in any kind of sexual relationship, this does not entitle you to engage in sexual activity with the other person/s without their consent. Even in marriage, sexual activity has to be consensual, and forcing your spouse or partner to engage in sexual activity is still illegal. Rape crisis phone lines and centres may be able to assist you if you are a victim of non-consensual sex. Men, women, transgender and intersex people can all be victims or perpetrators of sexual assaults. There is nothing to be ashamed of if you are a victim and, if the perpetrator suggests that it is your own fault, do not believe them. This is a common ploy to try to ensure that the crime is not reported.

Some countries have better reporting and prosecuting systems in place than others. You may wish to discuss with a rape crisis counsellor the pros and cons of pressing charges against the perpetrator. If you have ever thought about committing a sexual assault, it is important to seek help from a counsellor, psychologist or psychiatrist to help you learn to express yourself in a more appropriate manner.

Some people will try to coerce someone to have sex with them. Coercion is where the person does not force you, but they make you feel that you have to. This is not OK either. If you have said no to sex, and the person you are with keeps trying to talk you into changing your mind this is not OK.

Even though sex is an activity that can be emotion free, for many people it involves them being emotionally and physically vulnerable. This means that after sexual activity you should always be considerate and kind to the person/people involved. The gender of the people involved is not relevant, emotions and a sense of vulnerability and/or connection are very personal and individual. For some people on the autism spectrum the sense of connect or disconnect that may be experienced during and/or after sexual activity can be both unexpected and powerful. This is one of the reasons why it is important not to try to coerce people into sexual activity or engage in sexual activity with people just because they said that they will like you if you do.

Often people who want to engage in sexual activity with you will tell you that if you do, they will like you more, or love you more. This is very rarely true, but it can be an effective way to coerce someone without them realizing they have been coerced.

Family members – sisters, brothers, parents, children, grandparents

Relationships with these people should always be non-sexual. It is illegal to engage in sexual activity with these family members. If you know of people who are engaging in sexual activity with any children you should report this to the police and/or child services in your area. Children need to be allowed to grow up into young adults before they engage in sexual activity. If any of these people ask you to do anything sexual with them, you should also report this to the police, even if you did not do what they asked. This is because this person may go on to do the same thing or worse to someone else.

Non-sexual relationships with family members can be complex and difficult, or easy, or a combination of these. Not all family members like each other or love each other. Some parents, grandparents and siblings are very supportive while others are not. There is a saying that 'while you can't choose your family members you can choose your friends'. Traditionally, society has encouraged people to be loyal and loving towards family members even when that is not reciprocated.

However, if you have family members that treat you very badly or continually put you down or disrespect you or your life, then it is important that you realize that you do not have to just put up with this. It is OK to move out of your parents' home and into your own or shared accommodation. It is OK not to go to family events and not to invite family members to events that you are celebrating. A particular form of manipulation that family members may engage in is called gaslighting. When a person is gaslighting, their goal is to create so much doubt in the minds of their targets that the target/ victim no longer trusts their own judgement about things and starts to believe the manipulator. The victim/target then falls under the power and control of the manipulator. Examples of gaslighting are:

▶ A person saying things with such an intensity that it appears they are convinced that their truth is the only truth. In this case the victim begins to doubt their own perspective.

▶ The abuser will state their position and vigorously and unwaveringly deny the victim's experience. Often this will be coupled with a display of righteous indignation by the abuser.

▶ The abuser will also bring up historical issues to make their point, but in doing so add in inaccuracies that the victim cannot prove are untrue, so they start to doubt their memories.

▶ The abuser will also talk to the victim in a way that is shaming and causes the victim to feel guilty.

▶ Sadly, some people have one or more parent or sibling who engages in gaslighting them. If this is the case for you, it is important not to doubt yourself, and to seek assistance to live a positive and healthy life. This may mean not having any further contact with your family, no matter how much they try to guilt trip you. The goal of a person who engages in gaslighting is to gain and maintain power and advantage over their victim(s). If they have to tell an outright lie about you as part of that, it does not matter to them. Your feelings do not matter to them; you are just a useful tool to them.

Chris: The lies were not even consistent, but no one else seemed to notice, I thought I was going crazy at one point. It was only through my wife pointing out the inconsistencies over a six-month period and talking to me about how much money I had loaned my brother because I felt bad for him, that I realized he was just using me and had persuaded the rest of the family I was a useless weirdo. My wife convinced me to stop loaning him money and to say 'I need to ask my wife' whenever he asked me again. After six months of that, he stopped asking. He is still mean to me, but less. My wife says it is because he has no power over me now. I feel sad because we are having our first baby and I would like him or her to have good relationships with my family, but my brother says autistics can't be good parents, so I think I need to stop seeing him. And I know that is not true because there are lots of autistic parents out there who do a great job! If he had said I would be a useless dad I may well have believed him...

A big issue for many adults on the autism spectrum that affects their relationships with family members is their autism spectrum diagnosis. For these adults, their families either don't accept or don't believe the diagnosis and/or blame everything on the diagnosis. Some examples are from Lara, Frank and Sam.

Lara: My family are fine with my daughter's autism diagnosis, but they won't believe mine! I am always ending up arguing with my siblings and my parents because they tell me I am just being rude or deliberately misunderstanding them. I don't know why they say this, especially when my sister is always swearing at me for not driving her wherever she wants to go. She says I should do this because she is family and she doesn't have a car, whereas I have a car and don't work so I should be available for her. In the end I had to tell her, I am not her slave and I have my own life. My parents took her side and said I was selfish, but my brother came over to talk to me and said he was sorry they were all using me. He said it was good that I had my own life and was studying to get a job so I could support my daughter more easily. Now, I see my brother but not the rest of my family. I think he hasn't told them he sees me.

Frank: I have really bad sensory sensitivities and this makes it hard for me to go out. I can get angry really easily if there are too many sounds I find painful, and I prefer not to get angry. My dad said I am just an idiot and that I should grow up and get a job. He says I am just pretending I can't stand the noise and that my autism isn't real. I live at home and unless I can get a supported job or accommodation, I am stuck here. My social worker has suggested that I take Dad to see her and she can try to help him understand, so I might do that in the future.

Sam: My mum and dad say that I shouldn't have kids because I will give them my Asperger's. They won't let me date anyone or go out to places I could meet people. I am not a kid anymore, but they keep treating me like one. Online friends have suggested I try to get a place at college to study and then I can live in student accommodation, which is really cheap. They said I have to act more grown up if I want to be treated as a grown up, and setting a goal of being independent means making small step goals along the way and keep working at it.

Some family members are really supportive and loving. You may live with family and be very happy. If you need a lot of support, one of your siblings may be planning to help you when your parents are too old to do this. Whatever you want, it is important to discuss this with your family long before it is an urgent issue. With some autistics able to access individualized funding, it is much easier to choose where to live and who will provide your support.

If you want to show your family members you love them and care about them, some simple things that you can do to show this are:

▶ Tell them you love them.

▶ Make them or buy them a birthday card and give it to them on their birthday.

▶ Give them a present, just because, occasionally.

▶ Offer to help organize or do things for/during family events/celebrations.

▶ If you live away from them, phone, text or contact them every week to say hello and ask how they are.

▶ If you live with them, help out around the house if you can. If you can't, just tell them how much you appreciate them.

▶ Say please and thank you.

▶ Smile at them when you first see them (once a day is enough).

References

Cloud-Townsend Resources (n.d.) *Video Advice*. Available at www.cloudtownsend.com/video-advice, accessed on 15 October 2015.

Jorge Cham (2013) *A Guide to Academic Relationships. Piled Higher and Deeper*. Available at www.phdcomics.com/comics/archive.php?comicid=1651, accessed on 26 January 2016.

5

Understanding Your Own Sexuality

Humans tend to develop an understanding of their sexuality some time after puberty, but for some people they are aware of strong attractions to particular people before that. It can be a confusing issue for some people and completely obvious to other people. For most people it takes a number of years and some sexual encounters (activity) to decide whether they would prefer to be sexually or emotionally involved with a man or a woman or a person whose gender is irrelevant. People on the autism spectrum can find it more difficult to understand their sexuality as it involves not just self-awareness but an understanding of others and how we best interact with and fit in with others.

In some cultures it is not acceptable to have sex outside of marriage. In most Western countries this is not the case anymore. Typically, these same cultures do not accept relationships other than heterosexual ones as equal to heterosexual marriage/relationships, although there are exceptions. In these cultures it can be harder to explore your sexuality or to accept it if it is different from the majority.

While you are learning to understand your sexuality you may start off thinking that you should be like everyone else around you. However, not everyone is the same. You cannot tell someone's sexuality by looking at them. In high school many high school boys and girls say that they are sexually active in heterosexual relationships. Most of these students are in fact lying. Students say this to look more adult as they think that this can give them status at school. Conversely and confusingly it can also lose them status. Teenage girls who get pregnant and have children while they are still of school age are more likely than their friends, who do not become young mums, to live in poverty and struggle to succeed in life.

Sexual attraction is a complicated thing: you know you are sexually attracted to someone because of the way you feel when you see them or are around them. However, you may feel excited to be around a friend, but not sexually attracted to them. If you like touch, you may want to touch particular people or feel very tingly if they touch you. If you do not like touch, then this would not apply. Sexual attraction is often described as an emotional response people experience when they find someone sexually appealing, where this emotional response leads to a desire for sexual contact with the person. Sexual attraction can be experienced towards any person and any gender, or even towards anything or even a concept. Sexual attraction can be in response to any of the qualities of a person; for example, a person's physical qualities such as appearance, movement, smell and clothing, or non-physical aspects such as their personality.

Sexual attraction can occur by itself or alongside other desires such as romantic and/or emotional. When someone experiences sexual attraction without emotional or romantic desire, it can result in that person only desiring sex and not a relationship. Sexual attraction is not the same as a sex drive, and you can have no current sexual attractions but still have a high sex drive, or conversely be very sexually attracted to a number of people but have a low sex drive, meaning that you do not want to have lots of sex with all those people who you find desirable. Desire and actioning that desire are two different things. It can be easier for some people on the autism spectrum to understand and experience desire than to work out how to take action to fulfil that desire.

If you have sexual desire but currently have no one to engage in sexual activity with, you may want to try giving yourself sexual pleasure. This is covered in Chapter 16.

In order to understand your sexuality you need to work out when you feel differently about people. When you are with your friends, you probably feel very comfortable and relaxed. When you are around people you don't like, you may feel tense, stressed and/or anxious. Strangely, when we are sexually attracted to someone we may feel anxious or tense also. Usually this is because we want them to interact with us but we are not sure. If we get to know them this anxiety and tension will ease, whereas the more we know people we don't like the worse this can get.

Another complication is that sexual identity/orientation is not always fixed for some people and can change over time. For example a teenager may identify as bisexual but as they get older see themselves as heterosexual and then in their mid-30s or 40s they may start to identify as homosexual. This is fine and nothing to be worried about. Equally, it is fine if your sexuality stays the same all your life.

Sexual attraction is thought to have biological, social and psychological aspects. Pheromones are a type of scent-bearing chemical secreted in people's sweat and other bodily fluids.

These are known to play a role in sexual attraction in other animals, and research is ongoing into their role in human sexual attraction. Social norms can influence what a society or culture deems sexually attractive, but they cannot make particular individuals sexually attracted to other specific individuals. For example, in some countries thin women are viewed as more attractive than more curvaceous women, whereas in other cultures the opposite is true.

Research in China (Zhang 2014) found that people with positive personalities are deemed more attractive than people who look exactly the same but are perceived to be less kind or caring. Most people are neither amazingly beautiful nor ugly, they just are. However, if you want to appear attractive to others, the cheapest thing that you can do to help this happen is to be kind and caring!

If you drink alcohol or use drugs, you will be more attracted to people when drunk/high than you would be if you were sober. In addition you may feel more attractive to others when you are drunk/high. In reality, this is the effect of the alcohol and not an actual increase in attractiveness on either side. Most alcohol and drugs have a negative impact on men's ability to have and sustain an erection, which makes many sexual activities more difficult and/or impossible for men in this state.

What sexual attraction looks like

If you are sexually attracted to someone you usually want to look at them more frequently than you would look at other people. You may like to look at a particular part of them or a particular piece of their clothing, such as a soft sweatshirt that they often wear. You should never take an item of clothing or any belongings from someone without asking their permission. Asking for an item of clothing or a belonging of someone that you are not in a relationship with can be interpreted very negatively by most people, so it is inadvisable to do this.

Often if someone is sexually attracted to you they will look at/make eye contact with you briefly, then turn away and then look back for longer. They may also look at you from head to toe slowly, this is often referred to as undressing someone with their eyes. When people do this they are often imagining what you look like naked, or what it may be like to touch your body. Having someone look at you like this does not mean that they will touch you or try to take your clothes off; it can just be a part of flirting.

People often stand closer to people that they are sexually attracted to – however, this does not mean that the person squished up next to you on the bus or train is sexually attracted to you, it just means the bus or train is full! If you are in a bookshop and looking at books and, when you look up, a particular person is looking at you and then they move closer, this could be them showing they are sexually attracted to you, or it could be that they are a shop assistant and think you need help!

Flirting is what someone does to show someone else that they are sexually attracted to them. However, not everyone who does this actually wants to have a sexual relationship with you. This is because some people just like flirting and in some cultures this is a normal activity that is done just to show someone that you appreciate something about them. Other parts of flirting are 'chatting you up', which is where people say particular things that indicate they are sexually attracted to you. These are usually context specific and culturally based. Very few people are obvious, and instead they use 'subtle' comments or phrases. It can be seen as rude or inappropriate to come right out and say that you would like to have sex with someone, although this does avoid any misunderstandings!

Ash: In recent years I've come to realize a lot of things about my youth. With regard to sex, relationships and boys/men, my inability to speak the social language was even worse than in other areas.

Before puberty, the thought of anything sexual was revolting to me. I actually felt sick if I saw people kissing. From the reaction of my peers I could tell that what I felt was not normal. Around age 12 or 13 I suddenly became very interested in boys. I had one crush after the next – and I was always madly in love and did stupid things to get in contact with the object of my infatuation. And to no avail. In the beginning I wrote love letters: 'Do you want to go out' – and the boy always said no. When I was 14 I had a big crush on a boy one year older. I spied on him, rang his doorbell and asked stupid questions when he opened, went past in the morning and asked if we should walk together to school, befriended his brother's best friend and asked him to ask this guy out for me. And the object of my desire was not interested. At all. He just said no, and politely rejected me. And I just carried on like nothing happened. Meanwhile, my friends started dating boys. My best friend, Ann, always had two or three admirers. She could pick and choose and very often she chose not to. I couldn't understand it. Nobody ever admired me – I had no offers. We were both good looking, wore the same type of clothes, and there was nothing (that I could see at least) that she had and I didn't.

Many years later I realized what it was. Ann spoke the social language of flirting: She acted a little bit interested, flirted a little, but not a lot, and when a guy approached her she seemed both interested and not interested – indecisive in fact – this way letting him take the initiative and also making her seem mysterious. I was just very bluntly interested. And I took initiatives when there was someone I was interested in. And it never worked.

I had relationships. Plenty, in fact. Every single one of them based on initiatives from guys I never took an interest in. Suddenly this guy showed up, started chatting and eventually we'd end up together. Most of them nice guys and we had a good time. Almost every time he broke up after a couple months. All the crushes I've had never became relationships. And it never occurred to me to change my strategy. In the 'dating market', there are some rules of the game, one of them being that girls or women don't reveal their true intentions, they just act mysterious and indecisive. I didn't know or understand the rules, so I never played by them. And therefore those boys that I was interested in were not interested in me.

When I was 19 I met S at a party. We talked the whole night and I told him to call me – which he did the following day. We walked for hours and fell in love, were madly in love for two or three months and then broke up. We both married someone else (I married one of those that showed up and started chatting...) and had children, got divorced and met again. And got married five years ago. My relationship with S is special in many ways. We are indeed a very good match. And our relationship is the first which is not based on him chatting me up out of the blue – because he actually had a girlfriend at the time we met – and it is not based on one of my fantasy crushes either. We both have a share in our first encounter, and in fact we both have a share in our reunion and marriage five or six years ago.

People can also wear particular kinds of clothes to signal that they are available for a sexual relationship and this varies according to context, culture and sexuality. Just because a female wears a very short skirt, does not mean that she is interested in having sex! Dressing to indicate sexual attraction is very complex and it is very hard to understand. Generally, if you want to indicate that you are available for a sexual encounter you would dress in a way that gives you confidence and you both look and smell good.

If you are going to a particular type of place or event you need to ensure that you follow the dress code. An example of this is a nightclub that may specify no jeans or trainers, in which case you would need to wear smart casual or smart clothes. Leather clubs may require leather and/or rubber outfits in order to be admitted. For older adults it is less important to wear particular types of clothes and more important to just look clean and tidy.

Some people are particularly interested in dressing up as characters or furries (animal characters), and they meet online or in real life at conventions or private parties. You can choose to dress up completely or to have a more simple costume. Some types of characters are anime, animals or movie characters. There are often specific rules around signalling sexual interest in these communities and they tend to be more open to people asking how to do this or being more blunt and to the point. It would be OK, for example, to ask 'can I scratch your back' at a furry event, and then, if the answer is yes, to do so. You could also be open about not having attended this kind of event before and ask what the rules are around interactions both sexual and non-sexual.

Dress codes for S&M (sadomasochistic) clubs and events are generally very strict and involve leather and rubber, and these do not indicate anything other than an interest in S&M. People in this type of environment tend to use explicit and easy-to-understand comments and language so that you will know if someone is sexually attracted to you. However, interest in this environment is often of a short duration and may not be continued beyond that initial encounter. This does not mean that the person does not like you, just that they were only briefly interested.

In some cultures, to show a small amount of skin around the ankle or wrist area is seen as being very sexual. It can be far more sexually attractive to be covered than in skimpy clothing in many places, and certainly warmer in cold climates!

Another complication is that some cultures are very specific about what men and women should wear, and in others people can choose how to dress. Subcultures such as younger adults or particular religions or groups who engage in specific activities can have unwritten dress codes – a dress code is what someone is meant to wear to belong to that group or attend an event. An example is a work uniform, while another example is being naked at a nudist camp.

You can ask some friends what clothes are appropriate for different contexts, but it can be difficult for some parents to discuss this with their adult children. If you do not have anyone in real life that you can ask, you may want to join an online group for adults on the spectrum and ask them what they think. Generally, other adults on the autism spectrum are non-judgemental and accepting of a wide range of genders and sexuality.

> Lynne: When I was a young adult, I used to go to nightclubs and I was always really uncomfortable and never knew if people were talking to me just to talk to me or if they were trying to indicate a sexual interest in me. I was really jealous of my gay male friends who would just be really to the point if they were attracted to someone and no one was offended by this. When I tried the same tactic, of saying something like, 'do you want to have sex with me?' I was told this was really offensive and I shouldn't do that. It was so complicated and I was told that the way I dressed in 'male' clothing indicated that I would be the person indicating attraction to people I was attracted to. However, I had no idea what my friends were talking about until I read lots of books on the subject. Then I realized that in

some subcultures, like lesbians, the way you dress can indicate a whole set of hidden things, like sexual activity preference. For me this was just so weird, because I like to wear things that are comfortable and this overrides any and every other reason to wear particular clothes.

Dave: I found that if I wore clean jeans and a smart polo-shirt or shirt, women were more likely to talk to me than if I had my comfy trackpants on. My friends had talked to me about making sure I was clean and smelt good and I found out that this was really important to most people I met. For a while I used to just spray deodorant on before I went out, but when I started to have a shower and put clean clothes on before meeting people, I noticed that people would stand closer and interact with me for longer. I also got my first girlfriend after I had been doing this for a while. I think it was because it took me a while to feel comfortable in clean clean clothes and my friends said they could see my uncomfortableness and it made other people feel awkward. Once I was comfortable, they were too.

If you want to increase your chances of being found sexually attractive the best things to do are:

► Be kind and caring.

► Show your sense of humour.

► Dress in clean clothes.

► Be clean and smell neutral or nice.

► Have brushed hair and teeth.

► Stand or sit up straight with your arms down (not folded in front of you).

What sexual attraction feels like

If you feel attracted sexually to someone there will often be a physical and/or emotional signal in your body. This can be obvious or more subtle, and will be specific to you as an individual and is often quite different for men and women whether transgender, intersex or biologically male/female.

Men, for example, may have an erection when they are attracted sexually to someone, although not every erection signals this. For example, waking up with an erection is quite normal and does not mean that you are sexually attracted to the person delivering the post who happens to arrive at the same time as you wake up. However, if a man is thinking about a specific person and they experience an erection every time they think about them, a reasonable explanation is that they are sexually attracted to that person.

Both men and women can experience 'butterflies', which means a weird feeling in the stomach/chest, when they are sexually attracted to someone. Other common gender neutral feelings are nervousness and/or anxiety around a specific person, thinking about someone for prolonged periods of time and wanting to meet up with and/or impress someone a lot.

Women can experience a sort of tingling sensation and/or they can feel their vagina becoming wet when they are very attracted to someone sexually.

Many people fantasize (think about in a sexual way) someone whom they are sexually attracted to when they masturbate. Masturbation is where you give yourself an orgasm, it usually involves touching your own genitals with your hand, although women may use vibrators or other sex toys instead.

If you are sexually attracted to someone you need to think about how to let them know. It is important to be respectful and try not to make the person feel uncomfortable when you do this. You should never follow someone in the street, for example, as this can frighten people and is illegal if done over a period of time (it is viewed as stalking).

In a bar or a club it can be acceptable to move closer to someone and, if they do not move away, to gently reach out and touch them; for example, on the arm or shoulder. Again if they do not move away then you can assume they are comfortable being close to you. At this point you could ask if you could dance with and/or kiss them. If they say no, this signals that they are *not* interested and you must respect this. If someone approaches you in this way and you reciprocate their interest, you can touch their back/arms/face when you dance with them or hold them as you both kiss. However, if you are not interested, you can just say no thanks and move away.

However, you should never approach a person who is under the legal age of consent in the country where you live, as in many places this is illegal and this applies even in the context of being online, where the offence is called grooming. If you are under the age of consent (which varies across the world from 14 to 21), you need to be aware that it is illegal for older people to approach you to request a sexual relationship and they would be breaking the law if they did have any sexual contact with you.

In addition, it is very important to understand that you do not have to have a sexual relationship with someone just because they are attracted to you or you to them. Sometimes the people we are attracted to sexually would make terrible relationship partners. We need to be aware of this and know the signs of a good and a bad relationship. Chapter 4 explains how you can tell if someone is a good friend or not, and this is a good place to start. You can also read Chapter 12, which talks about how to know when to end (or not start) a sexual relationship with someone.

However, the most important point is that if someone is negative, unkind or puts you down verbally, ignores you or acts as if you belong to them, this person is *not* someone that you should get into a relationship with. Many adults on the autism spectrum assume that other people are good and kind, and we believe what they say. Although this is the case for many people, it is not true for everyone. Some people will tell you that you will never find anyone who loves you for who you are, but they will have a relationship with you and you should be grateful. This type of person is *not nice*. Do not get involved in any kind of relationship with this kind of person.

People who are very controlling of what you can do or wear or say or where you can go or who you can talk to can be very dangerous, and often go on to be violent and aggressive to their partners. You should *never* have any kind of relationship with this kind of person either, no matter how much they might say that they love you, they do not: they just want to control you. These are early signs of an abusive person and there are a number of others such as coercing (persuading) you to have sex with them, isolating you from other people (family and or friends), intimidating or pressuring you to do what they want, being derogatory and/or physically hurting you. Abusers can be old or young, from any ethnicity and culture and any socio-economic group. They can also be any gender, as can their victims.

> Lynne: I met this really beautiful teacher; she was just lovely, with a beautiful smile and intelligence. At the beginning things were fine, but once I moved in to her home, she became very controlling. I had read about and seen things about family/ domestic violence on television, but I didn't know women could

be abusive. I knew that if a man ever hit you, you should leave the relationship straight away, but when she hit me and told me it was my fault because I had done something wrong I believed her. Even after my boss asked me how I got my bruises I didn't realize the relationship was unhealthy and that I should leave. In fact I never left, she got bored of me and threw me out with one small bag of clothes. It wasn't until my friends found out exactly what she had been doing and saying that I understood it really was not my fault, she was just manipulating and controlling me. I was really lucky that my friends let me live with them for a while or I would have been homeless. I was a nurse, I am intelligent and yet I couldn't see the signs. I look back and I realize that I just didn't know that it was an abusive relationship because she kept telling me she loved me, so somehow I just thought that was the important thing and everything else was just how it was.

People on the autism spectrum can be vulnerable to abusers because we don't always know that it is not OK, or that we have other options, or that we are not such terrible people that it is abuse or being alone. We are different and we may or may not be beautiful or handsome, but we can find friendships and sexual relationships that are positive and healthy and bring us joy, if we start to accept who we are and know that we are worth spending time with and being treated well.

What sexual attraction sounds like

It can be difficult to understand the difference between being given a compliment and someone trying to 'pick you up'. Pick you up, in this context, means to try to engage in some kind of intimate act with you. One way to try to make sense of this is to look at the context.

In general a compliment will be specifically about something you do or are wearing and a pick up line (comment designed to indicate sexual attraction/interest) will be more around what you look like or may be like in a sexual situation. If you compliment someone, and are not wanting to indicate sexual interest, you need to make sure that you are using polite language and a neutral tone of voice. You can smile in either situation. An example of the difference is shown below:

> Compliment – 'I really like your dress,
> where did you get it from?'

> Pick up line – 'What a gorgeous dress,
> you look really sexy in red.'

It is usually inappropriate to engage in explicit sexual conversations in the workplace. Instead people who are sexually attracted to each other will engage in more subtle flirting, which can start with compliments and then become a little more sexual. If you are unsure if someone is interested in you or not, one of the best ways to find out is to ask the person if they would like to go out for a drink with you. If they say yes but then invite a number of other people, this signals that they like you as a friend and are not interested in a sexual/ intimate relationship. If they say no, not on that day but how about a different evening, this usually means that they are busy on the requested evening. If, however, the person says yes and does not invite anyone else, they may be interested, and if the evening is enjoyable you could ask them if they would like to go out for dinner with you or go to a movie, as these are common activities for a date. Dates are the getting-to-know-you phase of a relationship that may become sexual/intimate.

If you are alone or with friends in a bar or nightclub type environment, it can be quite anxiety provoking wondering what to do and trying to work out if anyone is going to talk to or otherwise interact with you. It can help your nerves to hold something in your hand – non-alcoholic drinks are just as acceptable as alcoholic drinks. Someone asking you if you would like a drink is 'chatting you up', which means that they are indicating that they would like to talk to you and possibly become sexually/intimately involved even if only briefly.

The idea of flirting can make people nervous; if you get nervous don't forget to stay polite and nice. Being rude is not helpful at all. You need to demonstrate an interest in the other person by asking them questions about themselves and listening to the answers if you are doing this in real life. You could be chatting by text, Facebook messaging or another form of online interaction.

You need to respond to what the person you are flirting with says or types. Flirting also involves being complimentary. Using a personal and relevant compliment is more effective at conveying your interest than a generic compliment, which can be perceived as meaningless. For example, to say 'you are so handsome' is not particularly meaningful, whereas to say 'I love your sense of humour' is much more personal and therefore more likely to mean something positive to the person.

Some people on the autism spectrum do not notice when people are flirting with them. If you are one of these people, that is fine. You do not have to flirt to make a connection with another person. You can be who you are and express yourself how you normally do, as long as this is respectful. You may want to just tell someone that you would like to get to know them better, or ask them to do a particular activity with you, for example watch a movie or play a game.

Nick: I meet people in Second Life. I don't have a problem talking to people there because it isn't really me or them, they can't judge me because they can't see how shy or awkward I am, they just see my avatar and that is what they interact with. I have some really good friends in Second Life. One woman and I have been chatting through our avatars for a few years. Our avatars are in a relationship now. This has given me confidence to talk to real women in real life, though I still worry that they will think I am not, I don't know, not enough.

In some cultures flirting (expressing sexual attraction to someone) is a part of everyday life and is not actually meant to result in anything other than joy and appreciation of the other person. However, in other cultures flirting is seen as highly inappropriate and unacceptable. In Anglo-Saxon and Celtic-based cultures flirting is used to signal sexual attraction and then, if it is responded to, is often the first stage in 'picking someone up'. This does not mean lifting someone up, but means getting someone to agree to date and/or engage in sexual activity with you.

In cultures where flirting is an acceptable part of everyday life it does occur in the workplace; however, in all other cultures it is inappropriate in the workplace and can lead to harassment charges and/or losing your job. Sexting (sending sexually explicit photos or texts) is not an acceptable way to flirt and in some places is also illegal. If you have been sexted you can choose to block the sender using your phone's call blocker, or your service provider can block the number for you. If the person has repeatedly contacted you in this way, you may want to contact the police.

Feeling asexual

Some people do not have sexual attraction to or feelings for other people and that is OK. The term for this is asexual. Society provides very mixed messages about sexuality and people can feel pressured to express a sexuality they do not have if they are asexual. On the other hand, some people, such as priests and nuns are expected to be asexual when they may not naturally be so inclined.

Whatever your sexuality, you do not need to express it at all times. For example, it would be inappropriate to talk about sexual things at work unless you work in the sex industry. This is the case even if you are asexual.

If you want a romantic or life partner and are asexual this is perfectly possible, though it can be difficult to work out how to discuss this with potential partners. Some people may still have a preference for a particular gender of partner even if the relationship is asexual and this is fine too. You can find other asexual people online if you want to explore this further in a safe environment. Be aware of cyber safety at all times (see Chapter 9).

Some asexual people are attracted to objects and have sexual feelings, such as having an erection or experiencing wetness in their vagina, when touching or looking at that particular object. This is less well accepted by society as it is not talked about often. This does not mean that it is immoral or wrong, just that many people do not know about or understand this, often because it is not something that they have experienced.

Jenny: I was never very interested in sex and physical intimacy as a teenager. I read in books about how people enjoyed it and were driven by it but I couldn't really see the point myself.

When I was 16 I had a less-than-consensual sexual experience with an older man. I decided I didn't like sex with men straight after that and I figured I must be a lesbian. Those were the only available opinions as I saw it. So I identified as a lesbian for a long time but it never seemed quite 'right'. On the rare occasions I had a girlfriend I was intimidated by the physical intimacy aspect. While women were less challenging as intimate partners than men I still found myself put off by things like kissing as I was repulsed by saliva. I loved being close to a woman in a non-sexual way but sex was something I was happy to avoid. I had a girlfriend for a while who had a history of abuse and also didn't like physical contact. This would have been perfect but sadly she was not a good match for me emotionally so we split up.

A couple of years ago I heard about asexuality. I hadn't realized it was a real thing. I started to piece together my experiences and realized that I was probably asexual. This does not mean that I do not like intimacy, just that physical or sexual contact is not something I am interested in. I would love to find an asexual woman to be my emotional, intellectual and spiritual partner. I am only just learning about what is 'out there' in terms of asexuality. I am relieved to find that there are other people like me.

Feeling heterosexual

If you feel that you are heterosexual it means you are attracted to people of the opposite gender to you; for example, if you are a man, you are sexually attracted to women. If you are transgender and heterosexual you may have been born a male but be attracted to men because you identify as female. However, unless you appear female to most people, in this instance you may be perceived as homosexual, which may make it harder for you to find a partner.

In most societies the majority of people are heterosexual and most media portrays heterosexual relationships. A traditional family had a heterosexual mother and father and the children were assumed to be heterosexual so that they would go on to reproduce the traditional family model. However, there are more depictions of lesbians and gays in the media, books and movies, and there are families where children are being brought up by two parents who are of the same gender (i.e. both male or both female). If you feel out of place in the company of someone of the opposite gender, this does not necessarily mean that you are not heterosexual; it may just be a part of your social difficulties associated with being on the autism spectrum. Some autistic people who are lesbian or gay are more comfortable around people of the opposite gender because they are not feeling awkward about how to express sexual interest or worrying about how to make new lesbian or gay friends that may or may not help them to meet a (sexual) partner.

As boys grow up, the boys who are gay can often feel more comfortable being around girls than around boys. Likewise, girls who are growing up into lesbian women often feel more comfortable around boys as teenagers and young adults. This is because of the intersection of culture and sexuality. For example, heterosexual men often walk differently to gay men and use a deeper voice when speaking. A young gay adult may feel different from these men and choose to spend time with female friends even though he is sexually more attracted to males.

It can be hard to tell if you want to be friends with people or if you are sexually attracted to people unless you have an awareness of what attraction feels like and possibly sounds like. For many people sexuality is not permanently fixed and can fluctuate so that at times they are heterosexual and at other times bisexual or homosexual. Research has indicated that adults on the autism spectrum are more likely to have a variety of sexual identities than other adults and this may be because we do not understand the social world in the same way as typical people. Many autism spectrum adults will fall in love with or be sexually attracted to a particular person rather than a gender and this is fine.

Tony: Growing up with in a family with lesbian mums, I always thought I was heterosexual. I found girls attractive and thought I wanted a girlfriend. Then, when I started work, I got a girlfriend, but it was really hard work. When I talked to my mum she explained that relationships are hard work, but that the good should outweigh the bad. I am thinking now that the person is more important than the gender; I need to be able to be comfortable with the person as well as all that relationship stuff.

Laura: I just assumed that when I left school I would get married one day and have kids, I never really thought about if it was an option or not. I really love my husband, we met at a games night. He is also an aspie and we just understood each other. I think that we both find each other sexually attractive, but that is not the most important part of our relationship. For me it just felt right to be with my husband, I feel at ease around him and not constantly worrying about what he thinks or what I might have done wrong or anything. It is wonderful to just be accepted for who I am.

Feeling lesbian/gay (homosexual)

Many people who grow up to be lesbian or gay report that as primary/grade-schoolers they had crushes on adults who were the same gender as they were. Crushes are not exactly sexual attraction as they seem to come before a person has fully developed their sexuality, but crushes can signal the direction this might take. Other people report having crushes on their best friend, though it can be hard to distinguish between a crush and an attachment to a best friend unless you have experienced both and could tell them apart.

As an adult you may know that you feel lesbian or gay because stereotypical roles for your gender make no sense to you and you are not particularly interested in reading about or watching heterosexual relationships. Lucy reported that others called her lesbian for many years before she realized that she was, and it was only when others in the English literature class at college talked about the heterosexual relationship between two characters in the novel they were studying, that Lucy understood her lack of interest was characterized by a lack of noticing.

However, many young people and adults on the autism spectrum do not subscribe to stereotypical gender roles, so that alone does not mean that you will be lesbian or gay. For that to be the case, you would also need to be sexually attracted to your own gender. For example, if you thought about who you might like to be in bed with and this was usually a man and you are male, this is a good indication that you might be gay. Another indication for a man would be that he has an erection whenever he is around particular men and he thinks about men when he masturbates.

In some communities and/or cultures there are cultural taboos around homosexuality and this can result in some internalized homophobia (fear/dislike of homosexuals) and/ or shame. However, it is widely understood that same-sex attraction exists in many species and is a part of the normal range of sexuality. If you belong to a community that does not accept homosexuality and you think that you might be lesbian or gay, it can be very difficult to talk about in a positive way within your community. In this case it is important to find safe spaces to explore your sexual identity. There are organizations that can support families to come to an acceptance of their family member's homosexuality; for example, parents and friends of lesbians and gays (PFLAG), which has groups in many parts of the world.

There are also lesbian, gay, bisexual, transgender and intersex (LGBTI) helplines and social groups online and in the real world. You can find these through Google searches.

Carl: When I was at high school, I got really interested in men's bodies – classical Greek sculptures and black and white photos of muscular men. Girls and women just didn't interest me, whereas I would want to touch men. I never did touch anyone at school because I was afraid of getting even more bullied than I already was. Everyone already thought I was weird and I had heard them use the words homo, gay, faggot with such hatred that I didn't want this for me. However, once I left school and discovered gay bars and gay books and gay photography clubs it was amazing. OK some gay men still thought I was weird, but mostly I was accepted and I could accept myself as gay. I still love men's bodies even though I do not have a partner at the moment. I know I am gay because I find men beautiful and women just don't interest me at all.

Felicity: I can still feel the first time a girl (we were 16) touched my skin, that skin on skin was so amazing. I had never thought about how it would feel to want sex, but when her hand stroked my tummy, it was like my whole body tingled and I just started to ache and ache. I recently read that researchers have found that when a woman is very sexually aroused and has not had sexual release through an orgasm she can get whole body muscle aches and pains, or just in her stomach and vagina and uterus. I had this for the first ten years of my sexually active life. Maybe because of being autistic and being touch sensitive I was more sexually excited than typical people, I don't know. It was weird though, such pain and such physical longing. Men have never had this effect on me, so that's how I know I am lesbian.

Feeling pansexual/omnisexual/bisexual

Some people are sexually attracted to particular individuals and not to one gender or the other. This may be because they themselves are of a non-binary gender (neither completely male nor completely female) or because they are more interested in internal characteristics of people than external ones. For example, if personality is far more important to you in a potential partner than whether or not they are female. This is quite common amongst autism spectrum adults, who relate to the social world in a different way from typical people and tend not to value one gender or sexuality/sexual identity above another.

Pansexuals and omnisexuals fall into this category of gender not being important in a future partner, whereas bisexuals are sexually attracted to both males and females. As these sexualities are less visible in society it can be hard to work out if you feel pansexual or bisexual. If you have had some experience of kissing (on the lips) people of both genders, you can reflect on your thoughts about the kissing. Did you feel any differently before, during or after? Did one make you feel more tingly in your body? Did one have very little emotional or physical impact on you? Did one or the other or both have an effect on your genitals? These are the sorts of things that can help you understand your sexual attractions and sexual identity.

> James: Growing up, there were gay men on TV and straight people. I didn't know about bisexuality until I moved to London as a young adult. There was a bi group that used to meet up and I went along one day because I just never felt like I fitted in with gay men or straight men, I never really understood either of them. When I did have a male partner, I also had a female partner and the same the other way round. I liked sex and

cuddles with both. As I got older, I was less sex focused and it became more about the person. I still like sex with people but I tend to be in more monogamous relationships now so it is more important that I get on with the person than it was when I was younger and having very short term relationships of a few months or even only a few hours.

Changing your mind

As teenagers grow into adults, sometimes their sexuality changes too. This can be because they were unaware of the options that existed and so had been trying to fit into a category that wasn't natural for them; or it can be because something different feels right for them now, where it didn't before. Other people cannot make someone have a particular sexuality – sexuality originates from within us and is a mix of hormones, other brain chemicals and the way we respond to those around us.

If you have been sexually abused or assaulted in your life, it can be very difficult to become comfortable and happy with your sexuality and to express that sexuality. If you are one of these people, then you may have found that you changed your mind about who you would be willing to have a relationship with to try to protect yourself from further hurt.

However, sexuality in itself cannot cause us pain (unless we accept the validity of unkind comments from others), what can and does cause both pain and joy are the relationships we engage in as we learn to express our sexuality in a healthy and positive way. It is OK to change your mind about your sexual identity and relationship status, though you should always try to treat others with respect and kindness, especially when explaining a decrease / change in sexual interest.

Hannah: When I was little, the story books were all about girls growing up, marrying the prince and living happily ever after, so that is what I thought would happen. I always wanted children too and so I figured that this was how that happened. In my family sex and sexuality were never talked about. I didn't know there were any other ways of being. I got married and had two kids. I love my kids to bits but I was never 'in love' with their dad. I just wasn't interested in sex with him, but that was what I thought wives did. When the kids were about 12 and 14 their dad told me he wanted a divorce and I just said OK. This mum from the kids' school asked me if I wanted to come to tea at her house while the kids played on the Xbox. I had nothing better to do so I went. She ran a lesbian book club and lent me the book they had just read. I couldn't believe women could enjoy sex. Even though I was getting divorced from my husband they let me join their book club (I love reading). Over the next year I got to be friends with one of the book club women and sometimes I would go to her house for dinner. When my divorce came through, I had to move out of the house and, because I didn't work, I didn't have a lot of money to look for somewhere to live. My ex-husband got nearly everything and I was getting pretty stressed and having a lot of meltdowns. This friend from book club said I could flat with her, so I moved into her house. She had room for the kids too on their weeks with me. I guess it was another year before we kissed, and about two more months before we had sex. It was amazing, like I was alive and all the insides and outside of my body were connected. I was middle aged before I found my comfort zone sexually, and I talk to my kids about their choices, how it is OK to be gay or straight or anything else.

Josh: I was at uni and got drunk one night and kissed my room mate. I had really fancied him for ages, he was just such a nice guy. We were in a relationship for the rest of the year after that, but then I am not sure what happened, but he said sorry he couldn't be in a relationship with me anymore. He got married about a year later. I chat online with him sometimes and he said that he really did love me and really felt gay, but then he just stopped feeling that way and now he just feels like he is straight. I guess sexuality can be fluid for some people, and for others it is more fixed, and for others they experiment before they figure out what they like. One of my Second Life friends is gay but he tried to be straight for about three years first, but he said it just didn't feel natural to him. I guess people are complex and sexuality and relationships are just complex.

References

Zhang, Y., Fanchang, K., Zhong, Y. and Kou, H. (2014) 'Personality manipulations: Do they modulate facial attractiveness ratings?' *Personality and Individual Differences 70*, 80-84.

6

Understanding the Sexuality of Others

Although it is not usually possible to work out the sexuality of another person just by looking at them, there are a number of contextual clues to work out if their sexuality is compatible with yours. If you are not interested in having a sexual relationship with someone, it is considered quite rude to ask them questions about their sexuality. If you are interested in a sexual relationship of any kind with another person it can avoid awkward conversations if you are sure they have a compatible sexuality.

For example, a lesbian is not going to want to have a sexual relationship with a male, a heterosexual male is not going to want to have a sexual relationship with another male. Some heterosexual men can become violent if approached in a sexual manner by another man. If you think you are a gay man, try to get to know other gay men in places where people are open about their sexuality. Confusingly, some people will describe themselves as heterosexual but engage in short-term homosexual relationships. This may be because they feel uncomfortable describing themselves as anything except heterosexual or it may be that they are just experimenting.

The workplace is not a safe place to try to find out others' sexuality as it can be perceived as harassment or bullying and can lead to you being fired. In other contexts, the biggest clue to someone's sexuality is their environment. For example, if you are female and you go to a women-only bar, the likelihood is that most women in the bar are either lesbian or bisexual/pansexual or omnisexual. However, if you go to a typical neighbourhood bar, most of the men and women in the bar will be heterosexual. It can be very dangerous for men and women to try to start a sexual relationship with someone of their own gender in this kind of environment. In addition, alcohol can make it more difficult to get to know someone and to remove oneself from an unsafe situation if this becomes necessary.

Transgender and intersex adults can also be victims of prejudice and stigma in public areas and sadly can be threatened with or become victims of violence if their aggressors are in a group and/or have had a lot of alcohol and/or drugs. It is not possible to tell if someone is transgender or intersex from looking at them, which means that they need to decide if and when to tell people. When they do tell people, they can experience a variety of reactions. It is important to understand that negative reactions are due to bigotry to not any inherent problem with being transgender or intersex.

On online dating sites people can lie about their gender and/or sexuality as well as other personal details. Some people do this to amuse themselves and others do it to lure people into unsafe situations where they can take advantage of them through sexual assaults and/or rape. It is very important to make sure that you practise cyber safety at all times and that when you meet someone in real life with whom you have been 'chatting' online before, that you make sure to let other people know where you are going, who you are meeting and when so that, if there is a problem, the other people can let the police know these details. For more information on this topic see cyber safety and dating safety tips in Chapter 9.

> Marg: I went through this highly sexualized phase when I was about 20, having sex with any woman that asked, because I just loved the way orgasms made me feel and connected me to myself and centred me. It was like the best self-regulation strategy I had found. I met most people through online lesbian dating sites and what I found most amazing was that 90% of the women were married to men and just wanted a bit of fun when their husbands were out at work. This suited me because I didn't want to live with anyone or have to chat on the phone with anyone over and over – I just wanted sex. I figured sex with women would be much safer than with men, but I still told my friend where I was going and asked her to ring me within three hours of my arrival at the address to check I was OK. She had instructions to call the police if I did not respond to the phone call. One time I had to answer in the middle of sex because I was worried if I didn't we would be naked and the police would arrive to see if I had been axe-murdered!

7

Sexual Relationships

Unless you are engaging the services of a sex worker (prostitute – male / female / transsexual – or rent boy – male), sex is free and it can be fun, pleasurable and help to build intimacy and connections between two people. For some people on the autism spectrum, sex can enable them to connect to themselves and their partner in a way that nothing else does. For other people on the autism spectrum, sexual activities can be very overwhelming or distressing. You may not know how you will react to a sexual activity until you are in a sexual relationship. You do not need to engage in any kind of sexual activity that you do not want to, no matter what anyone says to you. If it doesn't feel right to you, don't do it.

Someone who has never had sex before is often called a virgin, and when you have sex for the first time it is called losing your virginity. In some cultures it is very important that this occurs on your wedding night. For many individuals it occurs some time between the ages of 16 and 25. If you are older than this it is OK to still be a virgin. If you do not want to engage in a sexual relationship that is OK. If you do want to, that is OK too. If you live in supported accommodation you have the right to engage in sexual relationships if you want to. It is important that you only engage in sexual activity with people who are above the legal age of consent. This varies between states and countries and can be different for heterosexual, lesbian and gay sexual acts.

If you are underage (younger than the legal age of consent), then it is important that you understand that some people will try to persuade you to have a sexual relationship with them. If someone a year older than you asks you to have sex with them this is different from if someone a lot older than you asks. A much older person who wants to have sex with an underage person is known as a paedophile, and they will often tell you to keep anything they do to you secret. Even if you think it will upset them, you must tell your parents and the police as the much older person is breaking the law. However, if you are under the legal age of consent, anyone that has sex with you of any kind is breaking the law, even if they are only a few months older than you and over the age of consent. An exception is in France, where they have a specific law concerning sex between two people who are between 15 and 18 being legal, but if a person is over 18 then their sexual partners must also be over 18.

Sexual relationships should involve both (or all) people feeling good about themselves and the other person/people. They usually involve kissing and touching of mouths and bodies including the sexual parts. How this touching and kissing is done varies between different people. Because sexual parts are involved it is important that you know where they are and what they are commonly called (see Figure 7.1). It is OK to ask if you can touch somewhere on someone with whom you are engaged in a sexual relationship. It is not OK to ask to touch someone with whom you are not in a relationship.

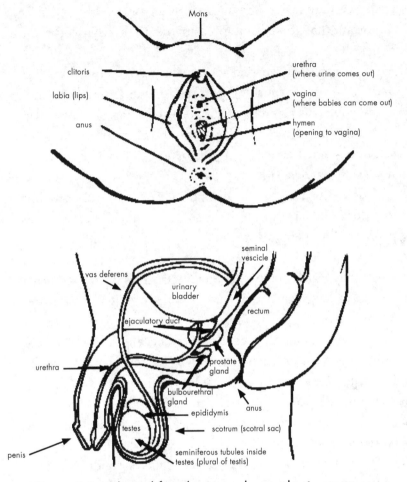

Figure 7.1 Male and female external reproductive anatomy

Feeling anxious about embarking on a sexual relationship is quite normal, so is a sense of excitement. If, however, you are very scared or feel threatened or coerced into sexual activity, it is important to know that you can say no. You never have to do anything sexual with anyone or for anyone, even if you are married to them.

The physical and emotional sensations that accompany sexual activity are different for different people. It is fine to prefer certain sexual activities to other ones, although it is important that you do not force anyone to do what you want either.

If you are very worried about what sexual activity will feel like, you can try touching yourself before letting a partner touch you. This could be as simple as working out what kind of hand movements feel nice on your arm to more complex sensations and actions like masturbation. This will be covered further in Chapter 16.

For many people the goal of sex is often orgasm but this does not have to be the case and is not the case for all people. How people experience an orgasm is individual, as is how they arrive at that orgasm. For males, an orgasm is when they ejaculate fluid (containing sperm) from their penis and is usually combined with feelings of intense pleasure. Women can get pregnant from sperm entering their vagina so it is important that condoms (male and/or female) are used to prevent pregnancy as well as protect against sexually transmitted diseases. If a couple is trying to have a baby, then they will need to have sexual intercourse without a condom to enable the sperm to enter into the vagina and travel up to the woman's fallopian tubes.

For a female, an orgasm is quite different and follows on from a huge amount of nerve and muscle tension, which builds up in the genitals, pelvis, buttocks and thighs of women when they are sexually stimulated. This tension is released through intensely pleasurable contractions, known as orgasm. A female orgasm is the intense simultaneous and repeated contraction of the uterus, vagina and anus. Some women feel this as one orgasm and others as different in the different places. Other women find it difficult or impossible to orgasm. Often when a woman orgasms her vagina releases more secretions and some people describe this as female ejaculation.

Some men and women climax or orgasm very easily, while others find it more difficult. Some people prefer to have one orgasm and others like to engage in more sexual activity following on from an orgasm in order to have another orgasm. Having multiple orgasms is where a person has two or more orgasms during a session of sexual activity. Sexual activity is covered further in Chapter 15.

Sexual relationships can be monogamous/closed, which means that the people involved agree to only engage in sexual activity with each other and no one else. The other form of sexual relationship is open, which means that the people involved agree that it is OK to engage in sexual activity with other people. However, some people assume that their sexual relationship is closed, but they have not actually discussed it and they find out that their lover (another name for someone you are having a sexual relationship with) is engaging in sexual activity with other people because they had assumed the relationship was open.

Polygamous relationships that have three or more members may also be closed or open. People engaged in polygamous relationships are often more upfront about sexual issues, although this is not always the case. For many open relationships there are a number of unspoken/unwritten rules which can be difficult for autistics to work out. Some of these can be:

▶ No sexual activity with other people is to take place in the main home.

▶ Sexual relationships with other people should be based on sex and not emotional connections.

▶ Be open about your primary relationship when meeting possible new sexual partners.

▶ Although honesty is vital, sharing details of your other sexual activities is usually not wanted (in some relationships the sharing of details is part of their relationship, whereas it can destroy other relationships).

▶ All sexual activity with other people *must* be done safely – using condoms and/or other barriers as relevant.

▶ No sex with mutual friends or co-workers.

However, it is up to those in each relationship to work out the rules for themselves. How this is done may change over time as well, what works when people are in their 20s or just at the beginning of a relationship may not work for them five or ten years later. Some examples of how this operated for two couples are given below.

Lucy: I thought I was bisexual and my husband was bisexual. We got married and it never occurred to me that we would have a monogamous relationship. In fact we never did. He used to drop me at my girlfriend's house and then go over to his boyfriend's house. We never brought anyone else to our home, but we did socialize with some of his boyfriends and their partners. I even got a job working for one of his boyfriend's partners once. It worked fine until I got emotionally involved with this woman and started to spend time with her that was supposed to be time with my husband. He talked to me about it and finally gave me an ultimatum 'her or me'; being an aspie, I thought he meant it and chose her. He explained later he just wanted me to see her less, which I would have done if he had said that. It can be quite hard being in open relationships if you are not really clear about the rules. I hadn't really understood that we were only supposed to be off with other people for three nights a week maximum.

Charlotte: My husband is gay, but we really get on well and both want to have children so we got married. He has a long-term boyfriend who is also married. This makes it easy for the guys as their families don't know anything except that they are 'certainly not gay as they are married'. However, over the years I have started to realize I got a bad deal: he goes off and has sex and I thought this meant I could have relationships too. But, because I am straight he said I can't because it would hurt him too much and it was different him seeing a guy than me seeing one. If I had known he was thinking like this I would have talked to him right at the beginning to say 'either we can both see other men or neither of us can'.

T.J.: I like open relationships because for me sex and love are two different things. I tell each new potential partner that I am only looking for a no-strings relationship and, if we do have sex, then I remind them after that I am not wanting a relationship, because I have one, but I am interested in having sex with them again. Of course if the sex wasn't good, then I don't bother with that! I just say goodbye.

8

Non-Sexual Relationships

Generally, most people do not engage in sexual activity with their friends unless they are friends with benefits/fuck buddies. Most of our relationships with other people are non-sexual. We go to work to work, to college to study and, although we can meet sexual partners in those places, most of the people we meet there we will just know as co-workers or peers and we will be friends with some of them.

Some people, especially those who are asexual, do not need or want sexual relationships with anyone. If, however, you do want a sexual relationship but are struggling to find a partner you can always gain sexual pleasure for yourself. It is OK to want, and OK not to want, sexual pleasure. See Chapter 15 for more information.

All relationships should be based on kindness towards, and caring for, the other person/people. This is the case for how you behave and how others should behave towards you. Within sexual relationships this kindness and caring is vital to nurture each other, as sex is often an intimate action that can make people feel extremely vulnerable. If that vulnerability is responded to with caring and kindness, it can forge a strong emotional bond. If instead the person is belittled and talked to negatively, it can cause feelings of shame, sadness, regret and even anger.

> Kane: My family treated me really badly, I had to do way more chores than my brothers and sisters and when I did finally get a job, I had to give my parents all my wages. It really sucked, so I decided to leave home. I moved into this friend from work's house. I rented a tiny tiny room that just had room for a mattress on the floor and was paying nearly all my wages for it. Then one night when I was trying to sleep I overheard my friend telling someone that it was so good 'Kane moved in, they are paying the whole rent, so I have lots more extra money now'. I was so pissed off. I thought that they were my friend but they were just using me, just like my family. I wanted to move out the next day, but I didn't have any money for a bond for a new place. Luckily I talked to this Asperger support group social worker and she helped me to get a place of my own because I was going to be homeless otherwise. I still get really angry when I see this person at work, but they don't know that I overheard them, so they don't know why I wanted to move out. They thought I went because I got my own place.

> Sara: I have been so lucky; people have been really kind to me over the years. Once a boyfriend came home with a new woman, packed some of my stuff into a plastic bag and threw it outside. He said that he bought everything else that was mine, so I couldn't have it and I had to get out because this new woman was moving in! I had to phone my friends and ask if I could stay with them until I found a new place to live. My friends were so kind, they came and picked me up and loaned

me clothes to wear until I got paid next. Since then I like to have a bank account that no one knows about where I save a little bit of money each week just in case something terrible like this happens again.

M.S.: I am kinda obviously a bit different, and even though I don't go around telling people I am autistic, most people think I am a bit weird before they even talk to me. I have found that people who turn out to be nice are the ones who try to get to know me without making judgements. They are also the ones who accept without comment that I only eat certain foods and only wear certain clothes. People who make stupid comments about my clothes or foods are not people who I am ever going to be friends with.

Many autistics have online friends, with Facebook being a popular way for people to make new friends online, through shared interest or self-advocacy pages. However, Facebook can at times be quite an uncomfortable place as negative or hateful posts can be made about you or in response to something you have said. Some people worry about blocking others online or on the phone but, if people are outright hateful or horrible, it is sensible to block them. In many closed and/or secret Facebook groups the exception is that you cannot remain a member if you block an admin.

Nathaniel Alderson (2015) suggests that blocking people is healthy and sends the message 'You are crossing my boundaries. I'm not going to let you do that.' He explains that:

If someone messages you on Facebook, and you ask them to stop, and they refuse to comply, then for the love of your own sanity, block them.

If someone is rude to you on Facebook, and after multiple attempts at trying to understand them, and they continue to be rude to you, block them.

It's your Facebook as well and you have every right to own your digital space. Would you let someone rude into your house? Blocking on Facebook is similar to locking the door on your house. DO IT it you feel unsafe around someone.

Misunderstandings of communication DO happen, and blocks can happen as a result, but the simple act of blocking will help calm things down. It's not the end of the world if you block someone! It's not rude to block them. And at the end of the day if you go without communicating to one person out of 7 billion, the world isn't going to end.

(Alderson 2015)

There are some very good reasons for blocking people, and it is important to understand that someone who behaves in the following way is not a friend and never will be. Friends respect each other's feelings and personal values and do not do things that have a big chance of upsetting or offending the other person.

Alderson (2015) suggests the following reasons to block someone; these apply equally if the person is not male:

If a guy messages you with pictures that you don't want, tell him to stop. If he doesn't stop, then block him. If the pictures are of genitals, and you don't have a relationship, report and block him.

If a guy sends you messages putting pressure on you to meet or doesn't listen to what you are saying about feeling uncomfortable, block him.

If a guy says inappropriate things, let him know they are inappropriate, and if he doesn't stop saying these things, block him.

If a guy gets ragey about things, and abuses you in pm, or is emotionally manipulative, block him.

In no circumstance or situation, do you HAVE to put up with anyone being mean or unkind to you. General guidelines of communication to follow is, if they are doing something that hurts you, or that you don't like, SAY SOMETHING ABOUT IT. If they continue to do or say something that hurts you, then take action. Block them if they show they are not willing to listen to you and respect you.

Abusive communication is abuse. Block abusive people. You don't have to put up with their abuse towards you. You don't have listen to ragers, or to manipulators, or deceitful people.

It is your Facebook, and you are in control of it. Stop allowing people to hurt you. If you say 'stop doing this hurtful action' and they don't respect that, then feel free to use block.

You will be called bitch, and other names, because of being assertive, but it is healthy for you to be assertive, and say 'No, I don't like this, this is not appropriate for me, I want you to stop what you are doing.'

It is healthy for you to stick up for your own boundaries.

However, it is also important to realize that friends can disagree about things without becoming abusive or unkind to each other. The disagreement may (in person) result in some shouting, but it should always be done in a respectful way that does not denigrate the other person. Friendships are not always forever and it is OK to stop being friends with someone if they become disrespectful, manipulative or unkind. It is also OK to make new friends, both online and in the real world.

If you meet someone and you seem to have a good understanding of each other and/or some things in common that mean you like to spend time together, then you could become friends with that person. Generally you should not message, text or call someone more than a couple of times if they do not reply to your texts or calls within a day or two. If you keep sending messages, texts and/or calling someone who has not responded to you, the person will begin to think that you are a stalker or too needy or desperate for them.

Non-autism spectrum people are often less intense in their interactions with friends and can find the intensity of people on the spectrum difficult. In addition, if they do not know that you are on the autism spectrum they may misunderstand and/ or be offended by your behaviour or actions from time to time. For this reason it can be useful to tell people your diagnosis, although some people can react quite negatively to hearing this and become unwilling to be friends. Even though this may feel hurtful, it is useful to remind yourself that someone who is unwilling to be your friend because of a word would be highly unlikely to be a good friend anyway. In slang terms, you might think 'it is their loss'.

As you get older, other people seem to become more accepting of invitations being declined due to tiredness or not feeling good. However, in your 20s and even 30s there can be an expectation that you should join in with everything your friends do, but you do not have to and good friends will be fine with this.

With your friends, you should let them know how you prefer to get in contact with them and communicate with them. If you like to text but not speak on the phone, let them know. If you are non-verbal and have a preferred communication system, good friends will want to learn how to use this communication system so that they can interact with you easily.

If your friends are also on the autism spectrum you can still experience misunderstandings, so it can be helpful if you think someone has been unkind or mean to check what they meant and to let them know that they upset or offended you and why this was the case. Friends who get really angry if you do this are not acting as friends and you might like to think about spending less time and energy on that person.

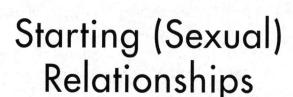

9

Starting (Sexual) Relationships

Online

Many adults on the autism spectrum enjoy interacting with others online as it takes away the complications of recognizing, understanding and responding to body language, tone of voice, etc. It can be easier to find people online who share interests and passions that you have, whether this is in forums, chat rooms, Facebook or arenas like Second Life.

In many ways it is simple to meet people online – as you use sites you start to see the same names over and over and interact with those people. Over time you build up your knowledge of who that person is in that context. However, it is important to understand that many people are not representing their true selves online and are instead pretending to be someone they would like to be or who they feel will help them to meet particular people. If you have never seen the MTV show 'Catfish', it is a good show to watch to illustrate this concept of people pretending to be other people online. People can pretend to be someone they are not when they are online for a number of reasons, but when they are pretending about this, they may also be lying about lots of other things in their life, and it is not a good start to any kind of relationship. Without some checking up online, like Google searching, image searching and regular videochatting, it is impossible to know if people are who they say they are.

However, there are also lots of people online who are just being themselves, and it can be a great way to get to know people slowly at your own pace. If the people you meet online interest you enough to want to have an online sexual relationship with them, that is fine. Many people have online sexual relationships where the sexual activity is limited to touching oneself and typing on a keyboard. Other people have their webcams on and/or talk about what they are doing to the other person. Be aware that this can be recorded and released into the public arena, which could be very embarrassing. It is also important to note that in some places sexting (sending sexually explicit photos via SMS or email) is illegal. Online sexual relationships with minors (people who are underage) is also illegal. If you engage in online sex through a paid site, the person you are interacting with will only be pretending to like you or love you because that is their job. They will not have real-life interest in you at all. Trying to contact them in real life could be construed as stalking and is a very bad idea.

If you have a Second Life character who becomes sexually involved with another person in Second Life, the other person is not interested in you sexually, just your character. It would not be appropriate to think that they are in love with you or that they are your best friend – their character is in a relationship with your character not you. Sometimes, people who have online avatar relationships do go on to meet in real life or through videochats as themselves. Some of these people manage the transition to good friends and a very few to real life sexual relationships, after taking time to get to know each other and not just each other's characters/avatars.

There are websites where you pay to watch people having sex (pornography). Some of these sites are showing people who did not give their permission and others are using paid actors or home videos where both people agreed. Some types of pornography are illegal and you can be arrested and imprisoned for having illegal pornography on your computer or other devices. What is legal/illegal varies between different countries/states. If you have a job or are studying, it is usually a breach of policy/contract to watch any kind of pornography at work/college/university. You can be fired or have internet access revoked in these situations. Pornography that depicts children or non-consensual sex acts is illegal, and viewing or saving images of child pornography can result in serious consequences including arrest, prison/jail time and being put on a sex offenders register for life, which restricts employment opportunities and housing options.

If you accidentally open up a pornography site on your computer at home, do not panic that you will be arrested! This is not likely, as people who are arrested for this sort of offence have usually accessed a large number of sites over a long period of time. The reason that they are arrested is that many countries have cybercrime police units. However, accessing legal pornography on your personal device outside of work is not an offence.

Research suggests that people who read or watch a lot of pornography begin to believe that ordinary people engage in sexual relationships like those depicted in pornography. Most people do not engage in most of the sexual activities depicted in pornography and the depiction of women in pornography has very little relation to reality. It has been found that people who read/watch pornography regularly can become dependent upon it and actually become addicted to pornography, which can stop them from being content or happy in a real relationship. If this is the case for you, addiction therapy has been shown to be helpful in moving forward to break the addiction and set realistic expectations for your life and sexual relationships with others.

Some people choose to use dating sites online to meet potential sexual partners, and this can suit some people on the spectrum. There are lots of dating sites, some of them are very specific in terms of religion or sexuality, for example, and others encompass everything, and advertisers and searchers specify what they are looking for. Some of these sites are free and others you either have to pay to join or pay to interact with other site members.

Dating sites that are specific to the type of person you are interested in are often easier to use successfully than big sites that have all kinds of people. For example, if you are a man seeking a man to have a sexual relationship with, you are more likely to find men who may be interested on a gay male dating site. The way the sites work is that people either write profiles that introduce themselves and what they are looking for, or they write a personal advert. Personals are the names for short pieces of text that explain who someone is and what they are looking for in a potential relationship.

If you use these sites, you may want to have an explanation of all the acronyms that are used. Acronyms are shortened versions of a phrase using just the initial letters; for example, swf is often used instead of single white female. Table 9.1 gives a brief overview of the most common acronyms and, as you will see, individual letters can mean different things depending on the letters next to them. It can be very confusing. It is OK to ask a friend to help you write a personal ad for an online dating site and to help you read some profiles.

Table 9.1 Online dating acronyms

420	This means the ad writer is a marijuana smoker, or into the cannabis lifestyle
A	Asian
Al	Animal lover
AT	'All that' – used to describe themselves as being everything that anyone could want – usually this person will be very egotistical
Alt	Alternative lifestyle – can mean anything, often used to indicate an interest in drugs or different types of sexual activity
B	Black
BB	Bodybuilder
BBW	Big beautiful woman – usually referring to women who weigh a large amount and not to breast size
B/D/S	Bondage/domination/submission – this person is into sexual roleplaying involving bondage and domination/ submission. There are large amounts of unwritten rules about this kind of sexual activity and it is best to read about these before trying to get involved in this with someone you do not know very well
BHM	Big handsome man usually referring to men who weigh a large amount
Bi	Bisexual
C	Couple usually refers to a couple looking for additional sexual partners. However, this can also be used to mean cute or Christian. Hopefully the rest of the ad will make it clear!
CD	Crossdresser – usually referring to a man who likes to wear women's clothes
D	Divorced
D/D Free	Drug and disease free – often used to indicate the person is HIV negative and does not use drugs

DL	Downlow is used to say the ad writer wants to keep this relationship 'on the downlow', private or discreet. Often this is used to imply the ad writer is already in a committed relationship and their long-term partner does not know about the ad. Some dating sites are specifically for married people wanting to have discreet affairs, such as Ashley Maddison
DTE	Down to earth indicates a relaxed personality
F	Female
FA	Fat acceptance often means that the ad writer likes overweight partners or that they are overweight themselves
FS	Financially secure/stable implies the ad writer has a permanent job or steady income
FWB NSA	Friend with benefits or no strings attached means the ad writer is looking for a casual sexual relationship and does not want to get emotionally involved. They may or may not already be involved in a long-term relationship
G	Gay
H	Hispanic
Hook-up	This is where two people meet up together, often to engage in sexual activity
HWP	Height/weight proportional suggests the ad writer is average height and build or is seeking an average sized person, as opposed to a BBW or BHM. This person is likely to be uninterested in you if you weigh more than average
I	Indian, meaning from India or of Indian descent
ISO	In search of/is seeking out is written before a list of what type of person the ad writer is interested in
J	Jewish
K	Kids – this means the ad writer has kids, or they are OK with someone who has kids. It does *not* imply a sexual interest in kids
L	Lesbian – although it can also be used to mean Latino
LDR	Long distance relationship – someone seeking this is not usually looking to have a live relationship but one that is mainly on the phone or online

LS	Legally separated means the person is married but planning to get divorced
LTR	Long-term relationship means the person is looking for a serious committed relationship
LD	Light drinker is often used to imply the person does not want to meet someone who drinks every day or gets very drunk when they go out
M	Male, although in personal ads for people seeking extra relationships to the one they are already in it can mean married
ND	Non-drinker
NK	No kids implies the person does not have or ever want kids
NM	Not married or never married
NS	Non-smoker – often non-smokers only want to meet other non-smokers
P	Professional
S	Single
S&M S/M	Both of these are used to indicate sadomasochism, usually one partner is the sadist (the top or dominant partner often known as the dom) and the other is the masochist (the bottom or sub). These sexual activities are role play with unwritten rules and codes. There are very good sources of information online if you wish to find out more about this type of sexual activity. It is important to do this before meeting someone who wants to engage in this type of sex
Tina	The ad writer is looking for a partner to use methamphetamine with
VGL	Very good looking – usually written by people of average looks who are seeking someone who looks like a model and who prioritizes looks over other factors
W	White or widowed, hopefully the context of the ad will tell you which
WAA	Will answer all (replies or inquiries) – usually this is seen as a sign of desperation and not as a sign of politeness

WE	Well endowed means the ad writer if male has a large penis, but if female that they have large breasts
Wi	Widowed
WLTM	Would like to meet
WTR	Willing to relocate – this can also be seen as a sign of desperation and usually people avoid replying to ads that seem desperate
X	Extreme – this is used to imply that out of the ordinary sexual exploits are acceptable or being sought

Examples of uses of online dating acronyms:

▶ *SBF WLTM L for NSA hook-ups – single black female would like to meet lesbian for no strings attached hook-ups – single black female is looking for a woman to have sex with but not for friends or a long-term relationship.*

▶ *BBW ISO SM for LTR – big beautiful woman is seeking single male for long-term relationship – overweight woman is looking to meet a single man to have a serious committed monogamous relationship with.*

The protocol for online dating sites is often to 'send a smile' or 'wink at' a person you think looks interesting or who you would like to get to know a bit more. If someone sends you a smile or wink it does not mean that they want to have a long-term relationship with you or engage in sexual activities, it just indicates that they would like to find out a bit more about you. When you get a smile or wink it is best to read the full profile of that person and you may want to use their image for a Google image search to check that they haven't stolen someone else's photos/identity.

Sending a smile back to someone is not enough, you also need to send them a message via the site if you would like to get to know them a bit more. Most sites have secure email systems so that your email address is not given out to people who are messaging you. This keeps you safe while you are trying to meet people that you don't know. If the person at this stage asks you to send them naked videos or photos or pictures of your penis/breasts/vagina, then it is likely that they are not looking for a long-term relationship. Sending them what they ask for is risky as it may be illegal where you or they live and they may then post those images to their friends or public websites. In addition, some people have been blackmailed and/ or lost their jobs because of the appearance on the internet of photos of them naked.

If you exchange messages for some time and think that the person is someone you might like to meet, it is a good idea to videochat with them first. This ensures that the person does at least look like they claim to look. Most people who lie about how they look are also lying about a lot of other things too. If someone refuses to videochat or tells you they don't have a webcam or makes other excuses, it is likely they are lying. In this case, it is probably best to give up on them and move on to try to meet someone who is honest and open about themselves.

Once you have videochatted with someone you may want to meet them in real life. This can be dangerous, so it is really important to have a safety plan. The reason it can be dangerous is that some people who are aggressive or sexually violent choose to meet people this way, just so they can harm them. For this reason you should always arrange to meet in a public place and you should always let at least one person know where you are going and who you are going to meet. Some people like to take a friend with them and the friend sits at a table or bench nearby where they can see and hear if you need help. This can be useful if, when you meet the person in real life, you find that you really don't like them, or that they make you feel very uncomfortable. You can then ask your friend to leave with you.

Some people choose never to meet in real life and just to continue to chat online, by Skype or on the phone. This is OK too. If you do choose to meet in person and the other person agrees, see Chapter 11 for more information about taking an online relationship into real life. If you have an online sexual relationship via Skype or other videochat systems it is sensible to angle the camera away from you before you remove any clothes and/or engage in any sexual touching as you do not want this broadcasting to anyone else at any point in the future (unless it is how you earn your living).

John: I like online dating – the old chat rooms were great because they were set up around particular interests and so you knew you would have something in common with the people in the chat room and so wouldn't need to make smalltalk. I mostly just keep my relationships online; it is perfect for me, though some people have wanted to meet or videochat, I just explain that I am not comfortable with that and it is online only or, if they don't like that, that's fine we can just stop having contact. Some people think that I will change my mind and they are quite surprised that I don't, but my social phobia in the real world is huge and I get so anxious I can't function, whereas online I can be me and I am quite funny and fun to interact with and have really intelligent conversations with too.

Aisha: I met the guy online, we chatted via the site messaging system and then he persuaded me to give him my phone number, so we could talk. I did this, but then he was expecting phone sex and I didn't even know what phone sex was. So I told him I had to go that there was someone at my door. I didn't want him to think I was an idiot or anything. Then I googled phone sex and read lots and lots about it. I wasn't sure how you were supposed to give yourself an orgasm and talk on the phone at the same time and that this talking would contribute to their orgasm. It all sounded very complicated to me, so I decided to think of it like a science project and break it down into different steps, and google each step too. I found out that phone sex can involve acting or actually doing and saying real things, which was amazing. I watched some documentaries on phone sex workers who were talking about touching themselves and sex stuff when they were doing the housework or typing up university assignments! I thought it was really interesting that when someone wanting phone sex asks 'what are you wearing' they do not actually want to know if you are wearing slippers, jeans and a t-shirt, but that they want to imagine you wearing nothing or underwear! Once I thought I had mastered it all I felt less nervous about the guy calling me again, which he did, and I did try but I think I got a few things wrong because I would answer honestly and he hung up on me and never called back.

Dating and hook-up apps

Dating apps are for people seeking more serious or longer-term relationships, whereas hook-up apps are designed to enable people to make contact based on very superficial characteristics, such as their photo and geographical proximity. Most people who use hook-up apps are looking for sex not a relationship. However, this does not mean that someone you meet via a hook-up app will have sex with you and you do not need to have sex with them either.

Hook-up apps – Tinder

Tinder is a smartphone application that lets people see photos and brief descriptions of other registered users in their local area. Tinder collates information about the user from their Facebook and Instagram profile and activities, including their photographs; it then brings up likely matches based on locality, mutual friends and other common interests. If you are using Tinder, to indicate that you are interested in a suggested match you swipe the screen right. Swiping the screen left tells Tinder that you are not interested in that suggested match. If you swipe right on a particular match *and* they swipe right on you, then you can chat to each other within the app.

Tinder is available in most of the world and in over 30 languages. Since the app launched in 2012 there have been more than 5 billion matches! There are paid and free versions of this app. It is important to be aware of safety issues around the use of dating apps like Tinder, with a high-profile alleged murder in Australia said to have been committed by a Tinder user who became frustrated with his match.

Hook-up apps – Bumble

Bumble is very similar to Tinder in layout and usage; however, it has one significant difference, which is that men are not able to initiate contact with women. Female Bumble users seeking men are presented with a series of matches, location can be selected from furthest away to closest, and you have 24 hours to initiate contact with any/all of the matches on screen. This restriction does not apply to users seeking same-sex relationships or friends.

Again, you should be aware of your personal safety when using Bumble as you cannot ever be sure that people you contact are safe.

Hook-up apps – Grindr

Grindr is a location-based social networking app for gay, bisexual and bi-curious men. Like Tinder, Grindr comes in both free and subscription-based versions. The app uses the smartphone satellite navigation system to provide the location of the user and then enables users to locate other men nearby. The user interface displays a grid of pictures of men, arranged from nearest to furthest away. Tapping on a person's picture brings up a brief profile for that user, as well as the option to chat to them, send pictures to them and share your own location with them.

Grindr is the largest and most popular gay/bisexual mobile app community in the world, available in over 190 countries. Over a million men use Grindr every day! Most users will be genuine but you should always be aware of the risks involved and ensure that someone knows where you are and who you are with if you do choose to meet up with someone through Grindr.

Dating sites – E-Harmony and Match.com

E-Harmony and Match.com operate worldwide but unless you and your match (assigned as a match by the site's algorithms) are both paid members, you cannot communicate easily or even see each other's photos. Users report that matches assigned by these sites do not match on some of the most important criteria, with some being provided with matches in different states/territories/regions when they had specified local only. Match.com has an information sheet about Asperger's. On both sites you need to select your gender and only male and female are offered, and also you can only pick one gender in terms of who you are looking for.

Like many dating sites, reviewers also note that a large number of profiles seem to be fake. Some of the smaller specialized dating sites do not seem to have this issue, but instead have a lack of members! Seeking dates via Twitter or chat rooms/forums is another option for online dating.

Dating site – Pink Sofa

Pink sofa is a web-based site where lesbian/bisexual women can post a profile (and a photo if they have a paid subscription). Most members are in the UK, USA, New Zealand or Australia. This site is set up for people looking for new friends and/or a new sexual relationship. Profiles stay up as long as you are a member and only paid members can message, free members can only smile/wink at people to indicate they would like more information. Information on profiles is generally clear and easy to understand with members introducing themselves and then what they are looking for. Many lesbians and bisexual women use sites like Pink Sofa to meet new friends if they move into a new area; however, there are also a significant number of women who have met their short or long-term partners online.

You can search by region and/or age and/or what type of relationship you are looking for. You can browse as a guest and you can also delete your profile at any time if you want to. You can choose only to view profiles of people online at the time and, if you want to instant message through the site, you can do that as well. The Pink Sofa also has a community section with events, accommodation listings, classified and 'chit chat', which is a hosted chat room for members. Many of these community sections are blank if you are based in regional areas rather than big cities. Cyber safety should always be considered on any dating site.

Dating site – Ashley Madison

This is a worldwide site for married people or those in long-term relationships seeking to have an additional relationship of any duration. Although some people criticize the site by saying that it promotes affairs which would not otherwise happen, there is no research on whether or not people who use the site would or would not have been in additional relationships otherwise. If you are seeking a relationship but do not ever want to live with a partner, then being an additional partner (mistress is a term often used for women in this situation) could work well for you. However, you need to be aware that these kinds of relationships can still be very complicated and messy, even if people say that they are only looking for some fun.

They have a large list of FAQs that can be accessed before signing up including the following details on safety issues:

> Never include your last name, email address, home address, phone number, place of work, or any other identifying information in your Internet profile or initial email message. Stop communicating with anyone who pressures you for personal or financial information or attempts in any way to trick you into revealing it. Use the service features offered on our system to help maintain your anonymity.

> If you choose to have a face-to-face meeting with another member, always tell someone in your family or a friend where you are going and when you will return. Never agree to be picked up at your home. Always provide your own transportation to and from your date and meet in a public place with many people around. (Ashley Madison FAQs, 2015)

Although Ashley Madison was hacked in 2015 and personal data relating to site members released, many of the emails were not genuine. Credit card numbers were also released, so it is worth only signing up to sites that you are OK with other people finding out about at any time in the future.

Cyber safety for dating sites and apps

It is really important to be aware of the safety issues around dating sites and apps. Most users are ordinary people but some users are dangerous predators. There is no way to know if the person you are interested in on a site is an ordinary person or a dangerous predator just from their profile or an initial interaction. For this reason there are a number of rules that you should follow to keep yourself safe when using dating sites and apps. These rules apply equally to men and women.

Do not share your login or password information

People can use your login and password information to hack your account and steal information from your computer. This is one of the ways identity theft can start. Computer hackers can also sometimes access your online banking and steal your money if they have access to your hard drive. You should never use common passwords such as Password or 12345 either!

Do not share all your personal contact details/identifying characteristics

You should not share your surname or contact details until you are sure the other person is trustworthy, which may not be until after you have met them in a public place. If you tell someone online all your personal details, such as your full name and phone number, or where you work or live, they could find you and arrive at your work or home when you do not want them to. In the worst case scenario they may stalk you or try to attack you. You should make sure your profile does not contain any identifying information.

You should not try to track down people that you have met online either. Checking out that they are legitimate by picture searching and Google is OK, standing outside their house when they have not arranged for you to meet them there is not OK, and can be seen as stalking and/or harassment, which are illegal.

Be aware of scammers

Some scammers use dating sites and apps to con people into giving them money. Ignore all requests to send money, especially overseas or by wire/bank transfer, and report the user who requested money to the website or app immediately. You should do this even if the person claims that they have had an accident or some other emergency, or that they only want to borrow money. In some cases the scammers will first send flowers or a gift or spend a number of months telling you how much they love you before asking you to give them the money to come and see you or for some other reason. These people do *not* love you, they just want your money.

Never give your financial information to people you have only just met or who you only know online. If you give people online your credit card details they may use these to buy lots of things, so it is important to be aware of this possibility.

There are some things that signal a person is a scammer, so you should block anyone who:

▶ asks to talk or chat to you on an outside email or messaging service within minutes of first contact

▶ asks you for money (report this to the site/app)

▶ vanishes mysteriously from the site, then reappears under a different name (usually because they have been banned in the first place for scamming or other dangerous behaviour)

▶ talks about it being destiny or fate that they met you

▶ asks for your address under the guise of sending flowers or gifts

▶ says things that contradict information they have previously given you (block and report this person immediately)

▶ sends you emails containing links to other websites (DO NOT CLICK ON THESE, they often contain viruses that can infect your computer).

The US Federal Trade Commission's (2011) advice to avoid online romance scams is a good resource to look at if you are concerned that you may be talking to a possible scammer.

References

Federal Trade Commission (2011) *Online Dating Scams*. Available at: http://onguardonline.gov/articles/0004-online-dating-scams, accessed 19 October 2015.

10

Sexual Relationships in Real Life

If you want to have a physical sexual relationship where someone else is touching you or being touched by you, then at some point in time that relationship will need to be in the real world and not just online. Some people prefer to meet people in real life rather than online because they want to see and hear the person 'for real' rather than getting to know a character that the person uses to interact with people online. Either is fine, it is what works best for you that it important.

How to meet people

Most people meet their future partners either at college or university or at work. However, there are a lot of other ways to meet people too. For example, if you belong to a church or a sport group, even if there are no single people there, the people there might know someone that you will like. It is OK to tell people that you are looking to meet someone to go out with, but this should only be done in certain places and ways. For example, in a church it would be inappropriate to say 'Let me know if you know anyone I can have sex with.' Instead you might talk to someone you know after church to say, 'I am thinking about starting to date. If you know anyone who you think might get on with me, could you let me know?'

In a sport group you might let people know that you are interested in dating, but don't know any single men/women/ people. Be aware that some individuals can be very judgemental about other people's sexuality so you need to feel safe before doing this. Joining an evening class to learn a new skill is another good way to meet people in real life. For example, you could join a Japanese language class if you are interested in Japanese. Everyone else there will also be interested in Japanese, so you already have something to talk about with the other students.

Other sorts of places to meet people are political or social justice organizations, special interest groups such as CosPlay/ historical societies or arts/craft groups, choirs, bands, theatre groups, book clubs, etc. You may have a local or regional autism spectrum social group. Some of these are run by, and for, people on the spectrum, and people come along and get to be themselves and be accepted for who they are, which encourages social interaction while minimizing anxiety. Activities in these social groups are as varied as the people who go along. You could even meet a future partner at a bus stop or supermarket!

> Janet: I belong to a church and when a new member moved to our church from another city, he sat next to me at the service. We got talking and I realized that he was also on the autism spectrum. We liked similar things and we can talk for hours and hours about these things. I asked him if he wanted to come and see my book collection and if he wanted to borrow any

of my books. He came round and we were talking so much that we hadn't realized the buses had stopped running and he couldn't get home. He stayed on the sofa and complained about how uncomfortable it was! After this we got together outside of church about once or twice a month and after a couple of years my parents asked him if he wanted to marry me. He said only if we lived in my apartment as his was even smaller than mine. We got married a few years ago and can still talk all day!

Josh: It is really hard to meet people because I am so shy in groups and have no idea what to say to each other. But I really love gaming and one of my gaming friends said he had a friend he wanted me to meet. He brought her over to my house the next weekend when we were having an all-nighter WoW session. She was really good at WoW. I don't think we actually spoke except about the game, but she just became part of the group and after a while asked me if I had Asperger's. When I said yes, she was like, 'oh OK, so does my brother, what do you like to eat?' She is quite happy with me not talking much and going to the McDonalds drive through to get chips. It is pretty cool. Then my friend kept asking me when I was going to have sex with her and I had no idea. I didn't know how to get from playing WoW to sex! After everyone left one Sunday, she just said, after McDonalds do you want to have sex? I nearly had a panic attack! I couldn't answer, but she said, 'It's OK to think about it, let's go get chips.' I just told her I had no idea what to do and she didn't care, she said we could just try to see what I might like doing, so we did.

Lucy: My co-worker kept wanting me to get a boyfriend, even though I kept telling her I didn't want one. When we went out after work for a meal one night, she brought this guy along and made me sit next to him. It was awful, I had no idea what to say to him and he kept staring at me. My co-worker just laughed about it at work and said she would find me a new blind date for next time. Now I have to keep making excuses to not go out ever with her in case this happens again. I don't know why she won't just accept me saying I don't want a boyfriend.

How to let someone know you are interested in getting to know them better – starting to date

If you have told other people that you are interested in dating (meeting someone with a view to a sexual/long-term relationship), they might set you up on a blind date. Blind dates are where two people meet up who have not previously met before, so they do not know what the other person looks like, which is why the term blind is used. These are usually arranged for people by either friends, colleagues or family. Most blind dates are not particularly enjoyable for either person.

If you have met the person before, instead of it being a blind date, it would be called a first date. (Nothing to do with calendars or fruit.) First dates are often equally unpleasant for everyone concerned. The reason first and blind dates are so difficult is anxiety. Both people are anxious about whether the other person will like them or not, if they will have anything to talk about, if they will like the movie/food/whatever activity they are doing and so on. People on the autism spectrum are used to living with this kind of anxiety, but for other people it can be incredibly stressful, as they do not usually think like this.

If you are going to go on a blind/first date you need to try to set it up to be as enjoyable as possible, otherwise you still won't know at the end of the date if you even vaguely like each other or not. Things to think about are:

▶ where to go

▶ what to do

▶ what time to meet

- what to wear

- how much it will cost (and who will pay for what).

For some people, ensuring there is wheelchair access or no bright lights would take priority, but for others the priority may be sharing an interest such as gaming or crafts. People usually have dates in the evening if they work regular hours (9am–5pm), so that they can go home, have a shower/bath, clean their teeth, brush their hair and put on clean clothes before meeting up at around 6 or 7pm. When thinking about cost and who will pay, this is a cultural thing, with men being expected to pay for the meal/outing for women in some places. However, it can avoid any problems to suggest 'going Dutch' when arranging the date. Going Dutch means that each person pays for their food/drink/ticket.

Typical blind/first dates might be:

- meeting for a coffee/drink at a café

- going to a restaurant for a meal

- going to watch a movie

- meeting up at an event and going around or watching the event together

- having a picnic

- going for a walk

- going swimming.

You should always ensure that you have a way to signal who you are meeting, by, for example, describing yourself as 'tall and thin with brown hair' and asking 'What do you look like so I will know who you are?' You may also want to exchange mobile phone numbers or friend each other on Facebook so that you can message each other if there are any problems getting to the venue on time.

Sometimes your date may not arrive; this does not always mean that they are not interested in you, although it can. It may be that they had a family emergency, or were taken sick or had to work late at work or some other problem occurred. If you are waiting for someone, after 15–20 minutes it is OK to call or message them ask 'Is everything OK? Would you like to cancel our date? If you want to have a rain check, that's fine too.' A rain check in this context means that you will meet up again, but not today. It is not OK to phone or message and be abusive, even if you are very frustrated. If the person does not text or message back, it indicates that they are unlikely to arrive.

Another good text to send is 'I am at the front door of... and I just realized that I might have got the day or time wrong, when are we meeting up?'

Some people are just late for everything they do and it is not personal, others will have been unable to come even though they wanted to, and yet others will have been too nervous to come and meet you, especially if it is a blind date. Occasionally a first or blind date just changes their mind and doesn't bother to tell you. There is no point in being really upset about this, it is better that you did not invest lots of time and emotional energy in someone who is inconsiderate!

The other way to start dating is to go to a speed dating event. These may well be very overwhelming for people on the autism spectrum but they do offer a way to briefly meet a number of people in one night and offer a good opportunity to practice talking to people. Speed dating events are run by various organizations and some community groups. They generally have very strict rules and the host or hostess for the evening would be happy to explain these to you if you ask them when you arrive. You could say 'Hi, I haven't been to one of these events before, could you please explain how it works for me?'

Where the speed dating organization has a website, this usually explains the process and registration details as well as any costs involved. Most speed dating is for heterosexuals, although some bigger cities, or gay/lesbian/bisexual/transgender/intersex groups may also occasionally have speed dating evenings.

Where universities are hosting PhD or thesis three-minute events or speed dating events, these are usually *not* related to dating in a relationship sense but are about networking to share research/try to obtain grants and/or work. So, if you are at university, try to clarify the agenda so that you do not prepare for the wrong kind of event. You could send the organizer an email to ask, 'Hi, could you just let me know who can register for the event and what they need to bring/do? Thanks.'

If you meet someone at a singles or dating event, and you like them and they like you, you can ask them for their phone number and/or give them your phone number or Facebook address or other social media connections. However, it is important to understand that when people who are not on the autism spectrum say that they will call/phone/text/message/contact you, this does not mean that they will. This would be translated to literally mean: 'I may or may not call you as I have not yet decided if I am interested enough in you to bother, but it is impolite to say this so I am saying I will call even though I might not.' If they do not call/phone/text/message/contact you within a week they probably won't, and this signals that they are not interested in dating you or having a relationship with you.

There are a number of unwritten social rules about how a date ends and the type of physical contact. It can be hard to know if a date is coming to its natural end or if the other person wants to continue to spend more time with you. If one or both of you have children at home, you might like to let them know what time you need to be home to let the babysitter get home, or you can ask them if they need to get home by [insert time] for their babysitter. Other reasons people need to end a date range from being bored to having to get to work, with all kinds of other reasons inbetween.

If you notice your date check their watch more than once within 10–15 minutes, they are probably wanting the date to end. You could say something like, 'Would you like to get going now?' If you are having a meal, once you have both finished your main course, you should ask if they want dessert or, if you do, say that you would like to see the dessert menu, and ask if that is OK with them. If you have been to see a movie or an event, once the movie/event is over then if you are wanting to go, that is fine, but you will need to say something and not assume that they are thinking the date is over too. You could say something like 'That was a great movie, thanks for coming to see it with me. I need to get going now, but I would like to see you again sometime if you are interested.' Of course if you did not like the date, you would not say that, instead you might say something like, 'The movie was good, thanks for coming with me. I have got to go now, thanks, bye.'

If you both seemed to enjoy the date, when you say goodbye it may be appropriate to ensure that the other person gets home or into their car or a taxi/bus/train safely. If you are out in the evening or dark, this is always a good thing, though you should ask, 'Would you like me to walk you to your car/taxi/train/bus/home?' If they say yes, then do. If you would like them to get you safely to your home or the transport home, you can ask them 'Would you mind walking me to [wherever you want them to walk you]?' Hopefully they will say they will walk you! If not, it may indicate that they are not interested in you.

Once you get to where you are going, then you need to decide how to say goodbye and what to do when you are saying goodbye. Traditionally, two people would kiss goodbye; however, it is more appropriate to ask 'would you like a kiss/ hug goodbye?' If you don't like kissing/hugging or don't want to do this, that's fine. However, if they ask and you say no, they may think you are not interested in them! If you have not told them about your autism/Asperger's diagnosis already, this might be a good time. You could say something like, 'I really enjoyed our date, and I'd like to see you again. I have Asperger's and I find hugging/kissing uncomfortable until I know people really well.' Or you could say, if they had asked if you would like a kiss, 'thanks, but I prefer hugging'. If you are fine with touch/kissing, then go ahead and enjoy it if the other person wants to too!

If you contact someone after a first/blind date or having met them at an event, you should wait until the next day to contact them. Your first contact should let them know that you enjoyed meeting or spending time with them and that you would like to meet up with them again. For example, you could text or message, 'Hi [their name], I had a great time with you yesterday, thanks. Would you like to [your choice of dating activity] sometime next week? [your name].' Many people choose to use emoticons and text speak when they message but it is fine not to do this if you are not comfortable with that.

If you have sent a message like this and you do not get a reply, the other person probably did not enjoy your company as much as you enjoyed their company. It is not OK to keep contacting the other person repeatedly. If you do this, it will make them dislike you. If you receive a message like this and you are not interested in pursuing a relationship with that person, then you should text back something polite but clear. For example, 'thanks, glad that you had a good time but I won't be able to meet up again'. If you choose not to reply, the other person will interpret that as you not being interested in them, but they may also decide that you are rude (even if the same person does not reply to other people and does not think that they are rude).

If, however, you did both have a good time and decide to go out again, that is great. It does not mean that the other person wants to live with you/marry you/and/or have sex with you. They may want to do any or all of these things but not for a while. Usually people date for a while before deciding if they want a serious relationship. For other people, they just drift into a serious relationship without either person thinking about the pros and cons of it. Many more people 'go out' for a while and then drift apart. If you are on the autism spectrum it can be very hard to work out how to make a relationship work, or even when you should leave a relationship. The rest of this chapter and Chapter 12 will give you lots of information about these complex life decisions.

Most of the things above apply equally to gay/lesbian dating and hetero/bisexual dating. However, gay men can be more open and explicit about their sexual interest in other men, which makes it much easier for gay men on the autism spectrum when dating. People who do not define themselves as male or female may also be more open about their interest but only if they feel safe.

When you get home from your date you should let your friends and/or family know that you are safe and OK. They may want to ask you lots of questions about how your date went, this is quite normal and it is up to you what information you choose to share. It is also OK to say that you don't really want to talk about it. If you say this, most non-autism spectrum people will think that you did not enjoy your date.

Tom: My sister made me sit next to her friend, Jamie, at dinner one night, even though she knows I hate talking to people I don't know. But her friend was really nice and she was interested in dog breeding just like I am, so we talked about her dogs and which dogs I wanted to breed. It was really great. When she left, she asked if I wanted to see her again and I said yes. Then my sister told me that her friend fancied me and that her question was like asking if I wanted to date her/get to know her to decide if I wanted to be her boyfriend! My parents were really cross with my sister because they said I am not capable of having a girlfriend when I don't even have a job, but my sister said I am, and I have a right to be happy and have a family of my own. I texted Jamie to ask if she wanted to go see a dog movie with me and she said yes. I think that I like her and she says she likes me. We are just dating at the moment.

Jackson: The good thing about being gay and going to a gay bar is that if someone asks me if they can buy me a drink, I know this is the signal that they are interested in me sexually. If I say yes, it signals maybe I am interested in them, if I say no, they know I am not interested but there are no hurt feelings. I have not had any long-term relationships because the men I have had relationships with have all broken up with me saying that I am too intense or too distant. I think that it is hard to be autistic and in a long-term relationship, but I am working on learning how to communicate with men in ways that they understand and being more open about my autism with someone if I think I want to be in a longer-term relationship with them.

Dale: I was always so nervous about meeting people in real life that I had met online, I figured that a train station was really public so I arranged to meet this man at the train station but I hadn't really thought about how to know for sure who he was, so I ended up going home after asking three different men if they were Daniel! Since he never contacted me again anyway I am not sure if he was one of those people and just thought he didn't like me in real life or if he was too scared to turn up and then too embarrassed to contact me again.

Nick: I really like this woman at my choir, she is so gorgeous. I can't stop talking about her. One of my friends says I need to ask her if she wants to go out, but I am too worried she will say no. I think she likes me. My parents invited her and her parents to our house for a BBQ and they all came and it was wonderful, but I don't know what to do next. We both live at home and don't drive so it is hard to work out what to do or how. I have been told to just ask her and then work out the problems, but I want to work out the problems first!

Negotiating the transition to a sexual relationship

If the person you have a date with asks you if you would like to go back to their house for coffee, this is usually an invitation to continue the date and possibly engage in some sexual activity. If you accept, this does not mean that you will have sex with your date. It means that you might. All people have a right to refuse sex whenever they like. This can mean, for example, that you could be invited in to someone's home 'for coffee' and be in the middle of undressing and they might say, 'sorry I can't', at which point you *must* stop, and it is nice to say something kind like, 'OK, no problem, would you like me to leave or would you like to just talk?'

If you meet someone at church the transition from dating to a sexual relationship may look very different to if you meet someone at a singles night at a bar. There are no exact rules to this transition and you may be asked if you want to fuck/screw/ have sex five minutes or years after meeting someone. If you believe that sex should be within marriage and you are dating someone who also believes this, then it is clear that for you as a couple, a sexual relationship will only occur if you get married.

However, for everyone else, it is a complex transition that is signalled by subtle or obvious clues.

> Lynne: I'm an aspie, and a lesbian. I'd been dating this woman for a while, I was very sexually attracted to her and I have a really high sex drive. I also know that I never notice if people are flirting with me and I just couldn't be bothered with all the misunderstandings that usually hound my attempts at dating. I prefer it when people are blunt, even if that can be hurtful at times. So anyway, I emailed this woman and asked her if she wanted to have sex the next time we met up. I didn't get an email back for what seemed like ages, though it may only have been a couple of days. She said yes and we did, but later she told me she was stunned and a bit taken aback by my approach. At the end of the day, I am who I am and if people don't want to be involved with me, I'd rather know sooner than later.

> Patti: In my experience, it is much easier to have a quick fuck with someone I just met than it is to date and then work out how to and when to go from dating to a full on sexual relationship. Mind you, quick fucks might be fun but they are just that, fleeting moments of fun and then nothing. It is the practical steps from sitting on the sofa watching TV to having sex that I just don't get. What magic signal am I missing?

When negotiating the transition to a sexual relationship, it can help if you already have some idea of sexual activities that you like or are interested in trying, as well as things that you know you do not like. In addition you need to think about where you are comfortable engaging in sexual activity in terms of place and time. Do you live by yourself or with someone else? Are you comfortable being naked or do you want to be covered by bedding or clothes? Are you going to be able to have your preferences in place or are you able/willing to compromise?

Are you and your potential partner planning sex or are you just hoping it will happen spontaneously? Does spontaneity stress or distress you? How are you going to manage your emotions if things do or do not happen in the way you are hoping for? Are there particular sensory aspects to a sexual relationship that are of concern to you; for example, do you and your partner need to have had a shower or bath just prior to and/or after, or do you need to be in a bedroom (yours or theirs) or do you not want to be in a bedroom? All of these preferences are intensely personal and may or may not be important to you or your potential partner.

For autism spectrum adults sensory issues can highlight experiences in both a good and/or a bad way. The more understanding that you have about your sensory preferences and dislikes, the more able you will be to discuss relevant aspects with a potential partner.

> Lucy: I like sex, I really do, and I am quite happy being naked, but I have a sensory sensitivity to light, particularly light bulbs. If a light bulb is turned on and catches my eye, it is like my eyeball is being burned. I have learned to make sure this can't happen as I have found that shouting 'Ah, my eye ball is burning!' ends any passion and sexual interest in the person I am with!

> Tony: I am sensitive to smells and I just can't have sex in a bed that is not clean, but also if the sheets have been washed in a strong smelling washing powder or liquid. In both cases I just get fixated on the smell and lose all interest in sex as I just want to get out of there. I found the best way to manage this and still have any kind of sex life is to only have sex in my house in my bed. I wash the sheets myself so I know they are clean and smell pleasant, which means I am not preoccupied with smelling sheets and so can focus on touch and feel and move more easily into sex.

If you think that you may want to be in an ongoing relationship (sexual or not) with someone, you may want to tell them that you are on the autism spectrum using words of your choice that you are happy with. It can be difficult to decide when to tell someone as, if they do not know you very well yet, hearing that you are autistic or have Asperger's can lead to a lot of misinterpretations or greater understanding. If the person already knows you well, they may be upset that you did not tell them before or they may not care at all! There is no right or wrong time, and sometimes people do not respond in accepting or positive ways. If the person changes how they interact with you, you could talk to them about this and see if it makes a difference. Don't forget you do not want to be in any kind of relationship with someone who does not accept you for who you are. This does not mean that you can be rude or badly behaved and that they should accept that, it means that they should behave the same way towards you before and after you disclose your autism/Asperger's.

Letting someone know you want to be friends but do not want to have a sexual relationship with them

Sometimes after a few dates or even if you have started a sexual relationship with someone, you or they may decide that it isn't right for you. You may just not enjoy the sexual side of the relationship or you may find the emotional or physical aspects unpleasant. It is OK to stop having a sexual relationship with someone or not to start one. If you want to stay friends, you will need to be careful about how you explain this to your girlfriend/boyfriend/partner/lover.

If you are already married and decide that you do not want to continue to have a sexual relationship with your spouse, this is OK, but your spouse may find it very hard to accept and be very hurt. However, it is much kinder in the long run to be upfront and honest. You may want to discuss it with a counsellor first and/or take your spouse with you to counselling to discuss this. For some people on the spectrum sexual activity does not become easier, nicer, more pleasurable; instead it can always feel awkward, unpleasant or just awful. For these people, instead of increasing intimacy, sexual activity can decrease it by increasing anxiety, stress and distress. The sensory aspects of sexual activity can be wonderful, neutral or horrid, depending upon who you are, who you are engaging in the sexual activity with and why. However, if you dislike it even with a person you love, in the comfort and safety of your own home, then it may be that you just do not like it, and that is OK. If this happens to you, talk to you partner, explain how it feels for you and try to find a way to help you both express your love in ways that are right for you both as a couple. Perhaps, for example, you could cuddle them while they masturbate so that they are still able to express their sexuality and you are able to stay in your comfort zone.

If you live with the person as their partner and have previously been sexually involved, they can react just like a spouse. They may, however, want to move out or want you to move out of the house once the discussion about you not wanting sex anymore has been had. If you choose not to be open with your partner and instead keep saying 'no' every time they ask if you want to have sex, it may take longer, but at some point they are going to get quite frustrated and possibly very upset or angry with you. People who live together often expect that the sexual aspect of their relationship will continue forever with the same intensity and frequency as their first few months, but this is rarely the case. Sexual desire and interest can fluctuate within a person and between people and this is quite normal. Ill health, tiredness, side effects of medication and stress are just some of the things that can affect sexual desire and performance.

There are a number of phrases in common use that mean the speaker does not want to be in a sexual relationship with you. These are often designed to reflect social norms but can be very confusing for autism spectrum adults.

> Di: This guy and I had a relationship for a few weeks then all of a sudden he said, 'I'm getting really busy at work, I don't think I can see you for a while'. I kept wondering when 'a while' would be up, so after one, two, six, eight weeks I would text and ask him if he wanted to meet up. He never texted back. I was so upset, I wondered what I had done wrong, but when I asked my sister she said he was breaking up with me! Another thing people say when you meet is 'I'll call you' or text, but then they don't. My sister said that people who say this rarely do call or text, it is just a politeness that is meaningless. I don't get it. If an aspie says they will call, they will unless their phone got stolen or broken and they couldn't find another one, or they got squashed or something terrible.

Other phrases are:

▶ You are just not my type – means I am not sexually attracted to you.

▶ It's not you, its me – means I want to end our sexual relationship (may or may not want to stay friends).

Sexual difficulties

If sexual intercourse (penetration of the vagina by a penis or fingers) becomes painful for a woman this can be related to vaginismus, which is a specific condition where there is an involuntary spasm/contraction of the muscles surrounding the entrance to the vagina when touching the area or attempting to insert anything (such as your own finger or a penis). Vaginismus can make penetration extremely painful, which can be very distressing and cause relationship stress. The level of pain is different for different women. Primary vaginismus is the name given where a woman has never been able to have pain-free sexual intercourse. Whereas secondary vaginismus is the name for the development of this condition after the woman has been able to engage in pleasurable pain-free intercourse at some time. Vaginismus can be treated by physical therapy and/or counselling.

The most common difficulty for males relates to problems getting an erection. Erections normally occur following sexual arousal, which activates a number of hormones, muscles, nerves and blood vessels. Nerve signals are sent from the brain to the penis, which stimulate the muscles in the penis to relax enabling blood to flow to the tissue in the penis. An erection occurs when the blood vessels in the penis are filled. At this point in time the blood vessels are 'closed' temporarily in the penis so that the erection can be maintained. Following orgasm, the blood vessels in the penis 'open' up allowing the blood to leave and the penis relaxes once again.

Many men occasionally have difficulty having or maintaining an erection, and this is quite normal. If you cannot get or maintain an erection that is firm enough to have sexual intercourse one time out of every four attempts or more you may have erectile dysfunction (ED), which can also be called sexual dysfunction. ED can be treated in most cases; help should be sought from a family doctor or specialist sexual health clinic.

11

Meeting Online and Then Transitioning to Real Life

As discussed in the online dating section, some people are not honest about who they are when they are online. For this reason, when you decide to first meet someone who you met online it is very important to make sure that you have a plan to meet them in a safe way. This means meeting in a neutral and public place, so not your home or their home or a place where you will be alone with them.

An example of a plan to stay safe when meeting someone in real life for the first time is to:

▶ Meet in a public place.

▶ Tell at least one other person where you are going and who you are going to meet. If possible ask them to meet up with you afterwards or to be at the same venue at the same time so that they can be there in case you need some support to leave.

▶ Do not drink from a drink that someone else gives you that you did not see being served.

▶ If you go to the toilet do not drink from your drink when you get back if you left it behind. Both of these points around drinks are due to the growing usage of the 'date rape' drug Rohypnol, which is colourless and odourless and is added to someone's drink so that they will become very drowsy and even pass out after drinking the drink. The drugger will often then sexually assault or rape the person that they have drugged. Both men and women can be victims of this kind of attack.

▶ Do not give the person you meet any money, although you can pay for any food or drink or activities that you do if you want to.

▶ It is better to meet the person a few times before you share more personal information like your phone number or address with them.

12

Ending Relationships

Not all relationships last for the rest of your life. Both good friendships and relationships can sometimes end due to conflict or difficulties in the relationship. Other relationships are really difficult or too intense and you or the other person may choose to end them as they are more negative than positive. Ending a relationship is often difficult and emotional, but for victims of family/domestic violence it can be a dangerous time. If you are in a violent relationship reach out to a women's refuge or domestic violence hotline; even if you are not a woman, these organizations will help you.

It is hard to end relationships in a way which ensures that no one is upset or distressed, but it is possible to end relationships respectfully. This opens up the possibility for you to be friends – if not immediately, then at some stage in the future. If your relationship ends and you did not want this to happen, it is OK to be very upset, but it is important to accept that the relationship is over and to realize that in the future you may meet someone who is more suitable and with whom you will have a much more positive relationship.

Ending online relationships

Ending online relationships can be really easy because you do not actually know the person in real life, so it may be as simple as blocking the person from contacting you. However, if you do this to someone they can be left not understanding why you blocked or unfriended them. If this happens to you, it can be quite bewildering and distressing.

It is socially acceptable to block or unfriend someone who has tried to harass or scam you or who has been disrespectful to you or about you. If, however, you have had any kind of positive relationship online with someone and then something happens that means you no longer like them, it is more socially acceptable to contact them privately via private message or email, for example, to say that you would prefer not to interact with them anymore.

There are exceptions to this; for example, if you have a Second Life relationship, you could just stop using that character and then the interactions will naturally cease. Another exception would be when a positive relationship becomes very uncomfortable due to the behaviour of the other person changing significantly, due to them, for example, requesting naked photos or sending you naked photos that you did not want. In this case blocking/unfriending is a good idea. You can also report them to the site owner. If their behaviour is very threatening or aggressive, you may want to notify law enforcement officials/the police too.

Sometimes when you end online relationships, people who know both of you online can 'take sides', which means that they decide one person is in the right and the other in the wrong and that they will only stay friends with one of the people. This may or may not happen to you. If lots of people react in a negative way to you because of an online breakup, it can be proactive to leave those groups/sites and join a different group/site. The person you broke up with may change their profile/avatar's name and try to get into a new relationship with you, so if you think that this might be the case you could block the new person too. Asking someone if they are doing this does not often result in a truthful answer, so there is not really any point in asking the person, though you could ask others who know him/her well.

Ending real-life relationships

In real life, relationships end for a variety of reasons and in a variety of ways; some of these are further explored in the next section. How the relationship ends can affect any future interactions you may have so, if you want to remain friends and/or you have children together, the relationship should be ended in as respectful a way as possible. For younger people or people in a relationship that has not lasted very long, breaking up can be less emotional, although for many people on the autism spectrum a relationship break up, whether non-sexual or sexual, can be very traumatic.

You can choose to end a relationship in person, or electronically – using voice or typed words. Societies typically judge the use of text or email (i.e. written communication) to be a less respectful way to let someone know you want to break up with them. Many people think it is better to break up in person, but this may feel too difficult or place you in danger, so there are many scenarios where sending a text or email to break up with someone is preferable.

Ending work relationships

If you are leaving your workplace, you should always prepare a written letter of resignation and then ask your boss/supervisor for a face-to-face meeting. At this meeting you should state that you are leaving and give them the letter of resignation. If they ask you why you are leaving, ensure that you have a polite and non-judgemental response ready. The reason that you should not say things like 'because this job stinks' is because that employer will be asked for a reference on your character and abilities when you apply for other jobs and, if you have offended them, they may be unwilling to recommend you for any other positions.

If you are transferring within the organization that you work or retiring, it is a nice idea to arrange to say goodbye with a small celebration for your current colleagues and boss. If you want to go to a bar/pub with them, then you could suggest that you all meet at a local bar/pub or a particular one that you like. However, if you do not want to do something like this, you can take a cake into work and put a card/note with it to say 'help yourselves, I've enjoyed working with you, but now I'm off to [wherever you are going]'. You can make your own cake or buy one, it doesn't matter. Doing something small like this can help other people to understand that you have appreciated them as well as showing that you are considerate.

If you are being made redundant, you may or may not want to do anything, and this is understandable and accepted by most people. If a large number of people are being made redundant, there is often an atmosphere of sadness or anger in the workplace in general. If others are being made redundant and you are not, it can be quite awkward as there can be some resentment towards people who have kept their jobs.

If someone else is leaving or transferring, there is sometimes a collection taken up to get the person a gift. Even if you did not like the person, you should put some money into the collection. If you do not, people will assume that you are rude, unkind and inconsiderate. Usually the collection is done using a large envelope and you either write your name on it or cross your name off the list if it is on it, add money and pass it on to someone else. Never pass it on to the person who is leaving because, even if they know that there is a collection for them, it is still supposed to be a surprise.

Other times that people may leave temporarily, such as to have a baby, adopt a child, have major surgery or go into hospital, are also events that sometimes result in a collection to buy a gift for the person. This is not done in the case of redundancy but is for people who retire.

If you are not leaving but you wish to stop being friends with a co-worker this can be very difficult to manage. If the relationship has ended because you both have just stopped talking to each other much but are still polite, neither of you needs to do anything. If, however, you have had an argument and have decided that you really do not like each other, you need to ensure that you are polite, otherwise it can create lots of employment issues and even result in formal reprimands or a loss of employment.

> Nina: I have always said that you should be kind to people as you build your career because you never know who you will come across on your way down! Also, when I leave a job, I try really hard to do so on a positive note. There is a saying that you should never burn your bridges, which in this case means making sure no one thinks badly of you when you leave, in case you ever need to go back and work there in the future. We never know what the future brings and people talk to each other about others, so there is a good chance your new boss will know your old boss.

Not all work relationships are difficult and it is possible to try to ensure that your work relationships are as positive as possible. The following guidelines could be useful if you want to ensure you get on with people at work:

- ▶ Be polite and use a calm tone of voice and try to make sure you do not appear to be shouting.

- ▶ Use people's correct names or forms of address (i.e. Mr Jones, Sir, Colonel Jones, Ms Black, Ma'am, Jo, etc.).

- ▶ Greet people with a smile, and the first time you meet people in a new workplace shake hands as you greet them by saying 'Hi, I'm [your name], I just started working here.'

- ▶ Sit near your co-workers on breaks or tell them that you are just going for a walk to get some fresh air.

- ▶ Stay calm at work. If you need to vent or let out some emotions, go to the toilet/bathroom – not to do anything in particular, just because this is a socially acceptable reason to take a short break away from other people. The walk to and from there will often be long enough for you to calm down again enough that you can manage the rest of the work day.

Ending friendships

Not all friendships are positive or healthy; some are toxic and abusive, while others just drift apart over time. Friendships mean different things to different people and, though some last a lifetime, this is less common than it was in stable and static communities. Society is more diverse and complex now, and the roles that people have within society are less stable than in years gone by. For example, it is now thought that most people will have at least 17 jobs in their working life, whereas in years gone by people worked in one company often at the same job, for their whole working life.

As people get older their interests and passions can change, you may or may not change, but most people who are not on the autism spectrum can change significantly. People who became friends at school may find that they just have nothing in common and no longer want to spend any time together. Usually this type of ending is gradual and happens with no formalities or external acknowledgement of the end of the friendship.

Sometimes when friends enter into new sexual relationships or start new jobs, all their energy is focused on that area of their life for a while. In these situations the friendship may or may not survive, or be wanted any longer. Again these endings tend to just happen and you might be left wondering if you did anything wrong. It is highly unlikely that you did, it is just that some people do not have enough time or emotional energy for more than one or two things/people in their lives.

However, some people turn out not to have been your friend at all, they were just pretending for their own benefit. See the section on emotional blackmail in Chapter 12 for further details on these sorts of people. If you realize that the person was not really your friend, you may choose not to have anything to do with them ever again, or you may choose to let them know that you no longer want to be friends. You can do this via text or email or on the phone. It is not sensible to do this in person as it could place you in danger.

Sadly some people who are friends become addicted to drugs, alcohol, gambling or other things, and it can be very hard to remain friends with an addict. This is because the addiction drives all the addicts' desires and behaviour, and they stop being the person who you became friends with and become enslaved in their addiction. If they do want to beat their addiction and seek support to do so, it is much easier to remain friends, but if not it can be impossible. Addicts can steal from their friends and lie to them as they seek out the means to satisfy their addiction. In these cases, it is likely that your friend will just stop contacting you except to ask to borrow money (which they are highly unlikely ever to pay back). It is important that you do not loan or give them money as you are enabling them to continue their addiction. It is fine to buy them a meal or a hot drink, but you may want to do this away from your home so that they are not given the opportunity to steal any of your belongings.

Many people believe in a social hierarchy and this can sometimes end friendships too. When a friend gets a big promotion or wins a lot of money, they can sometimes decide that you are not suitable as a friend. They may start to behave unkindly or inconsiderately towards you, or they may just stop contacting you at all.

These are the easy-to-end relationships because it is clear that the relationship is over; however, in some cases it is much harder to work out whether your relationship is positive and healthy or unhealthy. In these cases, the first thing that you need to do is objectively evaluate your friendship, which can be both easy and difficult. It is important to try not to get fixated on all the tiny details but to come to an overall evaluation.

The following set of questions will help you decide whether your relationship needs to end or if it could work well:

▶ Evaluate – are you unsure because of one incident or lots?

▶ If you have disagreements/arguments, are these because you both disagree with each other or because you refuse to agree on things?

▶ Does what you argue about mean more to you than your friend? For example, if you argue about something that is a fundamental belief to one of you, can you resolve your differences and get along or not?

▶ What does it mean to you to be around the person – are you more or less anxious around them? Do you find yourself more or less happy/sad/frustrated after spending time with them?

▶ How do you feel when you want to spend time or chat with your friend but they are not available? What do you think and feel about the reasons they give you?

▶ Are they manipulative or abusive to you or anyone else?

▶ Do you share any interests or enjoy doing anything together?

When you have completed your evaluation, you should be able to tell if your friendship is good and worth working on or if you need to end the friendship. If you decide to stop being friends, it is OK to just stop interacting with the person, or you could let them know that you feel that you are not able to be friends with them anymore.

Sometimes, it is possible that you treat a friend badly or are manipulative towards them. This is not acceptable behaviour and you should ask yourself why you are behaving in that way. What is it that you want out of life and how could you go about that more constructively? If you are more negative to someone than positive, you are not being their friend and you should either stop behaving in that way or stop contacting them.

Another issue that is quite common for autism spectrum adults is that other people can misinterpret behaviours including communication being misunderstood and make assumptions about the intent behind actions, etc. The ways that neurodiverse adults make and sustain friendships can be quite different to typical adults, and the ways they communicate can also be quite different. Most typical adult friendships are based on spending time together, and this may or may not involve a shared activity. Many typical friendships involve a lot of communication, often including gossiping/chatting about other people that the friends both know. In contrast, many autism spectrum friendships are based around a shared interest or commonality and most interactions are grounded in that interest or commonality.

Typical friends expect there to be a large element of emotional reciprocity, meaning that they expect you to share your life events and emotional states with them regularly and they expect you to be interested in their life and emotions. Interest includes sympathy and empathy as well as emotional support. Practical support may or may not be expected, whereas most neurodiverse friends prefer to offer practical support. Good friends may feel that it is OK to wake each other up in the middle of the night if they are very distressed, whereas this is definitely not OK for other friends.

Many people on the autism spectrum are assumed to be too intense or alternatively too detached, and many behaviours reinforce these views. For example, texting a person more than four or five times a day can be interpreted as too intense, but not phoning more than once a month can be viewed as too detached. It is important to let people know if you are not sure how much contact they are comfortable with, as it can be too complicated to work out before annoying the person so much that they decide that they do not want to be friends with you!

> Adam: When I meet a new friend I want to text them all the time. Every time I think of something that I want to share, I type out a text and hit send. I was about 24 and someone told me that

they found it really annoying to be constantly interrupted by my texts. After I thought about it for a few months, I figured out that maybe that was why so many people that I thought were friends would avoid contact with me after a few weeks. I asked that person if this could be the case and they said 'yes, if you keep on texting, people either figure you are crazy, stalking them or that you are too high maintenance for them'. I wasn't sure what high maintenance was, but I didn't want to look stupid so I asked my brother and he said that it meant that the other person thought I would be too intense and too much hard work to bother with. I don't get why no one had said that to me before and my brother said that people probably didn't want to upset me, especially if they thought I was a crazy stalker!

The rigid autistic thinking style can be hard for typical people to understand and they can sometimes think that you are being difficult or just wanting to boss them around. If you want to stay friends with typical people, it can help to explain why you are asking for particular things without using your autism spectrum diagnosis as an excuse.

Nick: I hate being late to get anywhere and I get really anxious if I am going to be late. When I tried to tell my flatmate, who is my best friend, that this was really upsetting me because of my autism, she said I was just using an excuse and I should just 'chill out'. She got really angry and frustrated with me for keep nagging her. In the end I looked up some videos on YouTube about anxiety and asked her to watch them with me, and I explained how I felt so anxious just with the idea we might be late, and then I got more anxious because I knew I was making her annoyed by asking her to hurry up, but I couldn't 'chill out' because I was already anxious. She was quite interested in anxiety and now she says 'I'm not ready yet, I know you are anxious, but it's not the end of the world if we are late,' which helps a bit.

Literal use of language can also be challenging for typical people who, although they may appreciate the honesty of autism spectrum adults, can also find it emotionally difficult. Unless you know someone really well or are really very good friends with them, it can be hard to navigate how to respond to some questions without upsetting your friends. In addition typical people can spend quite some time on smalltalk/social exchanges before they will talk about anything indepth or interesting, whereas autism spectrum adults tend to skip all the smalltalk and get straight to the point, which can make typical people feel uncomfortable.

Another problem that can occur is that some people may say mean things (true or untrue) about other people, but then become angry with you if you say other true things about the same person.

> Lucy: My friend has a difficult time with his family; they don't understand him or his Asperger's at all. They can be quite unkind, except for his sister. His sister is quite nice and we started to be friends, but then one day after she had been saying how unkind their dad was to my friend and I agreed and explained something I had seen him do that was really mean, she got really angry with me and won't talk to me anymore. She said that only family members could talk negatively about the family and I shouldn't do that. It makes no sense to me at all.

If a typical friend asks your opinion on any aspect of their appearance, they are rarely seeking a truthful answer, which is confusing for those on the autism spectrum and can lead to friendships ending if problems around this happen frequently.

> Claire: When I go shopping with my mum, if she asks me if I like a dress on her I can just be honest, she wants me to do that and it is easy, I don't have to think about it. But...when I go with

my partner, if she says, 'does this shirt look good on me?' and I answer honestly she can get really upset, so I try not to answer at all until I can remember what I have read online about how to answer these kinds of questions. Apparently if I say it looks bad, my partner is hearing YOU look bad...and they say aspies are literal! Honestly, I am saying the shirt is ugly or doesn't fit right, NOT you look ugly – she is beautiful.

Typical people may be happy to spend time involved in your special interest, or they may prefer not to. They may expect you to do things with them that you find uncomfortable and, unless you tell them that you don't want to and explain why, they may assume you no longer want to be friends if you don't attend these things with them.

James: I sat next to this girl at uni, she kept asking me to go to parties or out for pizza with her and some other people. I hate pizza and I don't like parties so I just said no or didn't turn up when she asked me to. After a few weeks she moved seats and stopped talking to me, which was sad because I really liked her. She was really nice. Now I know that I could have saved the friendship by telling her that I hate pizza and parties and thanking her for the invitation, or telling her 'thanks but I can't make it'.

However, there are people who will like you for who you are and for whom you do not have to make excuses or explain yourself. These people will make great friends. If you argue with this kind of friend, it will be OK to ask what you did that upset or made them angry and ask how you can fix it. For people who only like you when you seem typical, trust, honesty and openness are less likely to happen. Many autism spectrum adults can feel that they are being criticized or told off when their friends are just making conversation with them. It can help to ask others what they think about what your friend said if you do not want to ask your friend. However, a friend who truly accepts you for who you are will be fine with you asking what they really meant.

When a friend criticizes, they can be trying to be constructive and this can be very difficult for some adults on the autism spectrum to accept, in the same way that it can be hard for these same adults to understand why a friend is hurt by an honest response to a question. Although all people experience emotions, the way these are experienced and the influence they have over actions seems to be quite different for typical people and neurodiverse people, and this can impact friendships and relationships when there is a lack of understanding of each other.

Ending sexual relationships

A brief sexual encounter does not require a formal ending, it may happen and then it is over, there is no need for any declaration that it is over. Sometimes people will say that they will contact you after having sex with you, but this does not always mean that they actually will contact you. It seems to be a socially acceptable way to exit a situation without hurting anyone's feelings. Except that if you do not know this, your feelings are likely to get hurt. It is more honest and upfront to say, 'thanks, that was nice, bye'.

> Di: I like having one night stands or casual sex with guys I just met, because once it is over and we both feel great I can just leave, no need for interactions or anything. We both get the sexual pleasure and I don't have to be social and they don't have to bother with any of that 'I'll call you' rubbish. I honestly used to sit by the phone waiting when a guy had said that to me when I was in my 20s.

Any other sexual relationship that has been ongoing (twice or more) may need to be more explicitly ended. You should choose how to do this by thinking about where, when and how it would be least hurtful for the other person. You may choose to end it because you do not particularly enjoy the sexual activity with that person or you just do not want to have a longer-term relationship. Both of these reasons are fine, but there is no need to upset or be unkind to the other person in order to end the relationship.

Sometimes the person will want to break up with you (end the relationship) and it could be for any number of reasons, including social or sexual incompatibility. When people are socially incompatible, it means that they do not feel comfortable around each other by themselves or in wider social networks. Sexual incompatibility means that the people do not share the same sexual desires and/or that their sexual activity together was not particularly pleasurable. For some people in long-term relationships, their friendship is far more important than their sexual relationship, but in other cases the sexual activity is the primary reason for the relationship.

Some people will be fine with a text or email saying something like 'thanks for the fun', but others will be upset by that. There is no good or perfect way to end any relationship and how you or they end the relationship will depend on many contextual factors such as if you are friends as well, or if you were involved in a purely sexual relationship. If you were friends with benefits, it might be that one of you has met someone who you want to be romantically/sexually involved with and, in talking about the new person, the implicit message is that you can no longer be sexually involved but that your friendship is fine.

Ending marriages/civil unions/civil partnerships

When you are in a legally recognized relationship, such as a marriage, civil union or civil partnership, there are a number of steps that must be taken to completely end the relationship. These steps vary from country to country to sometimes differ according to the type of relationship. It is important to get independent legal advice around ending this kind of relationship to ensure that you are able to access things to which you have a legal right.

If there are children and custody issues involved, you may also like to contact an autism advocacy agency to get some support on how best to deal with the issues involved. Some countries have traditionally had a very negative view of the ability of adults on the autism spectrum to be effective and good parents, but this is changing to a more nuanced and realistic viewpoint.

Legal advice can be obtained for free or minimal cost in most countries and often the first appointment with a fee paying service is free. Be sure to check this before you go to the appointment if you are concerned about the cost.

Ending legal relationships can be very stressful, time- and energy-consuming. Some couples manage to end things amicably and sensibly, while others can become quite vicious and horrendous. Just because your partner says they will be amicable, does not mean you do not need legal advice.

> Lucy: When my ex-husband and I were getting divorced he said he would be reasonable and that we could file for a no fault divorce and just split stuff up by who it was meaningful for or who paid for it. But then his work colleagues kept telling him to take everything. Because he asked me to leave the house and I did, I lost a legal right to the house. And then he said he wanted to file for a fault divorce, which is where the 'other people'

involved get named too. This really annoyed me, because he had been having other relationships too, not just me, and his colleagues didn't know about his, just mine. I stayed very logical about it all, I didn't get vindictive or anything but I just pointed out that if my 'others' were named, then so would his be and he might find that embarrassing. He finally agreed but then refused to pay anything towards the divorce, even though he was earning money and I was at uni and had no income except for my part time odd jobs. I paid for it and, because I couldn't afford a lawyer and I didn't know about the free or low cost law services, I lost everything except my clothes and teddies and books, because I had taken those when I moved out.

John: My ex-wife wanted everything, she was entitled to half but not of my pension or stuff. Her lawyer kept sending these letters with demands and it took forever to agree. In the end I just said I was over the stress and I didn't care anymore. My lawyer made me sign a piece of paper to say I had ignored his legal advice and was giving up too much, but I just wanted it over. My mental health was worth more than the cost to replace lost things.

13

Reasons Why You Should End Relationships (How to Know a Relationship is Bad)

Autistic spectrum adults are overrepresented in domestic/ family violence statistics, and this chapter aims to prevent people ending up in a situation of domestic violence and to ensure that you have the ability to recognize an abusive partner. There are other reasons why you should end relationships and they will be briefly presented.

Your partner has an addiction

Some relationships can survive one of the people in it having an addiction, whether to food, gambling, drugs, alcohol or something else. However, many relationships cannot or should not. If your partner's addiction is placing you/the family into serious debt or danger or preventing you from having a positive relationship and your partner will not seek help to manage their addiction, then ending the relationship removes the risk and/or difficulties from being your issue or problem.

Addicts can continually promise to improve, do better or get help, but unless they actually do, the negative effects of their addiction will just continue. Many gamblers can spend, not only the family savings, but they increase debt dramatically by taking out and using a large number of credit cards. If you want to try to ensure your relationship survives, you may want to look in your local phone directory or google support groups that relate to your partner's particular addiction. You can also ask a local community service provider if they know where you can get some support and/or where your partner can get some help.

If your partner has a drug or acohol addiction, their behaviour can change as they become more and more addicted. As your partner becomes more focused on drinking or getting their next drug fix/hit, they will be less emotionally invested in the relationship and less interested in you. Any arguments or conflict that arise between you as a result of the drug/alcohol addiction will cause both of you more stress, and this additional stress will often increase your partner's drinking or drug use. In other cases, the addict will lie to cover up their addiction and this lying can erode the trust that was built up over the relationship.

Some drugs and alcohol can affect sexual function; for example, causing loss of libido (sexual interest) or erectile dysfunction. Where the substance does not have this effect, it can sometimes increase sex drive and/or lead to casual relationships with others due a decrease in impulse control.

Where this is the case, the addict will often forget to engage in safe sex and can therefore place their partner at risk of sexually transmitted diseases.

Often treatment programmes for addiction include the partner and, where they do not, there is often a separate support group for family members if they wish to join. If your partner does not fully engage with their treatment programme and you are struggling with the choices around ending or continuing your relationship, you could seek out relationship counselling. If you do this, you may need to ask a number of therapists about their knowledge of the autism spectrum and if they have experience supporting adults on the autism spectrum. This is because therapists with no knowledge of the autism spectrum may misinterpret your ideas and/or behaviour and be unable to communicate effectively with you.

You and your partner no longer like each other

Love is a mysterious thing that is undefinable in many ways, but it is less necessary in a long-term relationship than like/ friendship. If you cannot stand being around your partner and dislike them, your relationship will not be bringing you, or them, any joy.

When you like people, you are more able to accept their quirks and ignore little things which they might do that you dislike. However, when you no longer like your partner, you will find that all sorts of things that did not bother you before become really irritating or annoying to you. It is often at this stage of a relationship that people start trying to modify or change their partner's behaviour.

It is still possible to improve a relationship at this stage, as sometimes this dislike of each other comes about because one (or both) of the people in the relationship does not like or accept themselves for who they are. When people dislike themselves it is very hard to truly like someone else, as it becomes too easy just to see the other person as better than you and, over time, this attitude can turn into self-loathing and/or resentment of the other person.

For autism spectrum adults, it can be very difficult to develop a positive sense of self and to value themselves and their personalities. It is especially difficult for you if you were bullied during your younger years or constantly devalued. Being on the autism spectrum is not shameful and it does not make you inherently less valuable than another person. If you do not like yourself it is very important to work on accepting yourself for who you are. You can choose to try to develop some aspects of yourself; for example, learning more strategies to manage your stress and distress so that you do not hurt others or yourself when you have a meltdown.

It is OK to seek out supports and help to develop new skills, strategies and/or knowledge. For example, you may want to learn to use another communication system because you are non-verbal when you are distressed. A speech language therapist may be useful in this case, or you may choose to contact your nearest autism spectrum adult group and ask if they have any ideas for you.

Peer support from other adults on the autism spectrum has been shown to be highly effective in helping autistic adults to improve their self-esteem and self-acceptance. Improving these can sometimes help to improve existing relationships and friendships. Occasionally, developing self-acceptance and becoming aware that you are a valuable human being with positive attributes and some support needs (just like every other person on Earth), can damage relationships, usually when your partner likes you feeling less than them. Being dependent on someone is not the same as being less than someone.

Practising mindfulness, which is being present in the moment and accepting your feelings and then letting them go in a non-judgemental manner, can help you to feel better in yourself and give you the confidence to communicate your needs and wants. It can also help you to find the clarity of mind needed to evaluate whether or not seeking relationship counselling or other types of therapy can assist you and your partner, or if you should just not be together.

This sort of decision is complicated by whether or not you have children and if you have a moral/ethical commitment to stay with the person. For example, some people who are married do not believe that it is acceptable to get a divorce. Other people choose to stay in a relationship so that the children can be raised by both of their parents. In this case, often the couple do break up once the youngest child has finished or is about to finish high school. This is only sensible if you are not arguing, or yelling and/or completely ignoring each other most of the time. Children, whether or not they are on the autism spectrum, can pick up on the emotional atmosphere in the house and they can become quite distressed when they sense continued emotional discord between their parents.

These children can begin to blame themselves for any problems their parents might have, and it is better to talk to the children about how much they are loved by both their parents and it is you and your partner who have issues with each other and not with them, your child/ren. Family or relationship counselling is a very good idea if you decide to stay together for the sake of the children. During this therapy/counselling, some couples rediscover all the things they liked about each other and are able to strengthen their relationship.

Other couples come to the realization and acceptance that they are fundamentally incompatible and should indeed end their relationship. Compatibility is a complex concept which describes the ability of people to be together in a way that is conducive to getting along. In terms of software/apps, compatibility is the ability for that software/app to work on your phone/tablet/laptop. If it is not compatible it will not work.

> Suzy: I got married really young, most of the people I worked with thought I was a bit weird anyway, but they seemed shocked when I got married, and one of them said that I was too young and that, because people change so much in their 20s, it would be hard to make the marriage work as we might change and grow apart rather than change and get closer emotionally. They were right. My husband was ten years older than me and he had quite a few friends, whereas I didn't really have any, just a couple that I knew from a social group. When my husband and I would go out together, I would just sit in the corner in silence while everyone else seemed to be having a really good time. I just didn't feel comfortable at all and wanted to go home, which really annoyed him. As I got older I decided to say that I didn't want to do these things, I wanted to walk in the mountains near our house instead or cuddle up with the cat. He just didn't understand and it seemed like I had to do all the compromising. He got more social and I got less social and then he sat me down one day and said he couldn't do it anymore – he was feeling guilty every time he wanted to go out and this was who he was. He said he had met a new woman who made him realize he needed to be with someone who was social and who was at ease in themselves and not so rigid in their thinking. Once we had broken up, which was really distressing and awful, but once it was over, I was so much happier. All the things I didn't like about him, like having to have the radio on all the time when he was home, opening the windows when the neighbours were being noisy, I didn't have to live like that anymore, I could live in a way that made me feel comfortable. I'm aspie and I need

peace and quiet, I am so much happier now. I would never have broken up with him because I made a commitment to stay together, but I couldn't do that if he wanted to end it, so it worked out well in the end.

Mike: We met online and seemed to get on well initially, but we didn't have a lot in common apart from both being on the spectrum. We spent about six months together and then we started to really annoy each other whenever we saw each other, even the clothes we wore made the other person angry. He was wearing wool sweaters and I find wool really itchy and, urgggh, just being near it is horrid, but he said he had a right to wear things that he liked. He hated my hat, which I wear all winter as I hate my ears getting cold, and he said it made him mad just seeing it. We also ran out of things to talk about together, his interest in buses was so annoying, even though it was his knowledge that helped us meet in real life as he could give really good instructions about which buses to get and when. We were just talking at each other and my brother asked me why I was still seeing this guy when we clearly had nothing in common and didn't actually like each other so what was the point? I hadn't thought of it like that, so I talked to John and he agreed. We still chat online together sometimes but I haven't seen him for about a year now.

Sometimes when couples start to argue frequently, the arguments become more and more frequent and often more intense and this can be misinterpreted as no longer liking each other. If you are bewildered about why you are arguing or you realize that your arguments are not actually about your relationship, you may want to seek out couples counselling with a therapist who has an understanding of the autism spectrum and how it can impact relationships. If you and your partner can really listen to each other and hear what the other one wants and needs for the relationship to be successful and positive again, then you can both decide if you can do those things or not.

Your partner is objectifying you

Anyone can be objectified by anyone else. When someone is objectified it means that they are being viewed as and valued as an object and not a person. It might be that you are viewed as very beautiful and your partner likes to show you off to their friends, which on the surface can seem nice, but does not value you as a whole person. Sexual objectification is a particular type of objectification where the person is viewed solely as an object of sexual desire rather than a person with feelings and desires of their own.

A person who objectifies others is unlikely to have a positive relationship with anyone as they will assume that they are superior and the other person is there purely to service their needs/desires. This sort of person can become abusive over time or can lose interest in you when they find someone else to objectify. It is not a good idea to enter into a relationship with someone like this and, if someone starts to objectify you over time, then this indicates a deterioration of the relationship and a lack of respect for you.

Your partner is emotionally blackmailing you

Many autism spectrum adults struggle to recognize emotional blackmail, which can often lead to continuing and worsening abuse within a relationship. Emotional blackmail can take place in any type of relationship at any time. When there is a single occurrence of attempted emotional blackmail occurring during a disagreement or argument and it is responded to in a way that discourages further attempts, then there is no need to end the relationship. If, however, emotional blackmail is ongoing, then the relationship is very unhealthy and should be ended.

Emotional blackmail is where one person in a relationship (of any kind) behaves badly but blames the other person in the relationship for that behaviour. In emotional blackmail, the person being blamed accepts that they are in the wrong (even though they are not) and so feels at fault. Feeling at fault, the person who has been wronged tries to make things better for the person who behaved badly.

An example of this is:

> Lucy: My partner would yell and scream and shout when she got drunk. I hate going to parties anyway, but every now and then she would convince me to go and then I would end up being yelled at all the way home about how I ruined her life, she was just having fun, blah blah. The next day she would say it was all my fault for being so uptight and, if I would just relax, we would have more fun. Then she came up with the idea that if I didn't like going to parties I could stay home and she would go with her friends from work instead. She would tell me she would be home by say 1am, then at 2am I would start panicking that she had been run over or something and I would call her up to see if she was OK. She never answered the phone, so I would panic more. When she finally got home at say 3 or 4am she would tell me that if I really loved her I wouldn't bother her when she was out having fun. I used to get so stressed and became convinced that I was this boring person she complained about until she left me. Then I had the time and space to work out that if someone says they will be home by 1am and they don't come home till 4am, they are just using you, they don't love you. All that emotional blackmail of 'if you really loved me' was hiding the truth of 'if I really loved you, I wouldn't behave badly towards you'.

Other examples of emotional blackmail are when people blame their partner for their own behaviour at work, in other relationships or even mundane day-to-day activities. This blame laying is an attempt to excuse their own bad behaviour so they can get away with that behaviour with no consequences. Another word for emotional blackmail is manipulation. People try to manipulate other people to gain power, security, money, sex or other advantages.

> Tom: My ex-wife worked at this company that only had male managers. She worked hard and was hoping to get promoted, but when she thought no one was looking she would be on eBay buying and selling things. When she didn't get her promotion because they said she was not focused enough on work, she blamed me and said it was my fault for not attending the office Christmas party with her the year before. I could see how illogical that was so I pointed out that perhaps it was her eBay usage on work computers and she lost the plot yelling at me that I was so unsupportive and I didn't love her. That wasn't why we got divorced though, she did apologize later and said she knew it wasn't my fault, she was just angry because she had really wanted the promotion. We got divorced because she blamed my Asperger's every time we had a disagreement and, in the end, one of my online aspie friends asked me why I was married to someone who hated Asperger's. As soon as he asked me that I got fixated thinking about all the times she had blamed my Asperger's when we had an argument even if it was about her spending too much money on eBay – like how is that about Asperger's? After about five months of thinking about this all the time, I went to see an advice person and she said that I could file for divorce.

> Sasha: My ex told me he was only having an affair with my work colleague and then my best friend because I was too intense and emotional and he just needed some fun, and that

I should just get over it. I hadn't known about the affairs until another colleague asked me if I knew. I was devastated, but I refused to accept the blame. I didn't make him have sex with those other women did I? I told him it was over and I wanted to be with someone who respected me enough not to run around having sex with anyone else.

Mike: We used to argue all the time about time. Because of my autism I like things to be just so, and one of the things that is important to me is to be on time. My boyfriend wasn't interested in being on time and so we were often late and then I would be really stressed and anxious and then melt down. He kept telling me that if I really loved him, I would just relax and go with the flow. I still don't know what he meant by this, but I do know he wanted me to change who I am but he wasn't willing to get dressed five minutes earlier to help me manage my anxiety. He left me in the end, saying I wasn't good enough for him but now I realize that he wasn't good enough for me. He was unkind and inconsiderate.

Belle: I am quite overweight and I love to cook, it is how I show people I care about them. My flatmate put weight on eating all the food I made, but then blamed me for making him fat. I didn't make him eat it! I was really upset though, because I felt he was saying fat is bad and I am fat. I don't know why he is still flatting with me. I think I need to start writing down what he says is my fault so I can look at it clearly and maybe ask my other friend to help me process it and see if things are my fault or if he is manipulating me.

Manipulation happens in the workplace, in shared homes, in residential care, in friendships, families and relationships. Many adults on the autism spectrum were bullied at school or even in their homes as they were growing up. As adults it is important to develop self-care and self-respect in order to understand that it is not OK for other people to pretend that they like you or care about you in order to get you to do things for them. People who manipulate you do *not* love you; they may not even like you, despite what they say.

> J.B.: John used to tell me that he loved me, that I was special. He was my brother's friend at high school. I was three years younger. John told me he would love me even more if I took this backpack to school for him and then take it to the shopping mall and give it to Mr Green at this particular shop door. When I asked him what was in the backpack he ignored me. I thought he really loved me. When I got arrested, the police refused to believe I didn't know that I had been carrying drugs and drug money between John and Mr Green for six months, but I never looked in the bag because John asked me not to and he acted as if I was so special to him, as if he really liked me.

> Lucy: My boss told me I would get promoted if I did extra work. So I did extra work. Then she told me I would need to do even more because it was important that everyone saw me being busy. It took me a long time to work out she was just getting me to do her work while she spent her days fixing up her CV and applying for jobs. I felt like such an idiot, especially when I lost my job and she got promoted for being so efficient and no one would believe that I had done all the work she said she had done.

If you are in a relationship with a manipulative person, it is probably a good idea to end the relationship, though you may want to seek assistance or counselling on the best way to do this. Manipulators can use fear, guilt or a sense of duty/ loyalty or other obligation in order to emotionally blackmail you into doing what they want, even before you realize this is happening. There are different types of emotional blackmail or manipulation:

▶ Punishers – 'my way or the highway' is the manipulator's motto. This is a tricky area, because so many autism spectrum adults would prefer that life be run on their terms; however, this should not be at the cost of other people's dignity, respect or rights and freedoms. Interestingly, this can be used against autism spectrum adults by the second type of manipulator.

▶ Self-punishers – suggest that their victim must be the fully responsible adult in the relationship and that the victim is to blame for anything and everything that upsets or bothers the self-punisher. In this case the manipulator could blame their autism spectrum partner for upsetting them by turning the volume on the radio down, for example, even though their partner did this because the radio would hurt their ears otherwise, which links to the third type of manipulator.

▶ Sufferers – these manipulators play the victim claiming that 'if you don't do what I want, I will suffer, and it will be your fault'. For example, if you don't buy me that shirt, I will be sad and it will be all your fault, even if they have the money to buy the shirt for themselves.

▶ Gaslighting – gaslighting is another term for manipulators of any kind, often used to describe people who combine a number of techniques to make other people feel bad and give in to their demands.

Many people can be manipulative when it comes to money and they may demand or pressure you to give them money. Some emotional blackmail is more overt and involves threats to try to make you comply:

Doug: I think women just see me as on open wallet because I have a job and I own my house and a car. They say things like, if you love me you'd take me out for dinner, then if I do they get worse and in the end they are telling me they will leave me unless I buy them whatever it is they want. Some of these women have had jobs and some haven't, but it makes me really angry that I fell for this a number of times.

It is important to understand the legal framework around relationships before you enter into a long-term relationship. In many countries a person with whom you live becomes legally entitled to half of the property, even if it was owned outright by you prior to the relationship, after a particular number of years. For some people, manipulation is a long-term game and they can live with you for a few years and then break up with you just so they can get half of your home and savings.

Lucy: I was living with this woman and she asked me to register our partnership. Soon after that she said she didn't want to live with me anymore but because we had a registered partnership she wanted half of everything even though I had been paying for everything for the whole time we were together.

Martin: When I broke up with my partner after five years I ended up with nothing. I didn't know that I was entitled to have something, because we were seen as defacto spouses and so our home was supposed to be relationship property. Because I was so distressed about the break up I didn't go and see a lawyer and so I ended up with nothing at all, and had to move home again to live with my mum.

Manipulative people often lack self-awareness and never blame themselves for difficulties in relationships, often seeing themselves as the victims. This interpretation can often lead to anger, aggression and even rage. With these types of manipulators, you could be placed at risk by trying to get them to recognize their own behaviour. However, with others, including those autism spectrum adults who may exhibit some manipulative behaviours, talking openly about their emotional blackmail of you can help resolve these issues and help you to improve your relationship.

The most important thing to do with any manipulator is not to accept the blame for their bad behaviour and then to do something about it, either leaving if that is possible, or getting help to manage the situation if it is not possible. If the person manipulating you is your support worker or any other type of carer, the police may need to be involved. See the section below on abuse for more details.

If you have been emotionally blackmailed in the past, there are a number of steps you can take to try to minimize the risk of this happening again. This is because it is harder to emotionally blackmail people who are confident in themselves and understand the difference between healthy and unhealthy relationships and who would prefer not to be in a relationship than to be in an unhealthy one. These steps are:

▶ Develop a positive sense of self – it is much easier to emotionally blackmail someone who feels less valuable than other people or who does not believe that they deserve to be loved. Being on the autism spectrum does not make you less lovable or any less deserving of a good relationship than anyone else.

▶ Learn how to say no – autism spectrum adults can find it really hard to say no to people, and manipulators know this and can use it to their advantage. It is perfectly OK to say no and it can help to practise this skill and learn to say no in ways that feel more comfortable for you, by, for example, saying: 'I'm sorry, I would like to be able to do…but I can't/I'm busy.' You do not need to give reasons for saying no, and people who pressure you after you have said no are giving you a warning sign that they may well try to emotionally blackmail or manipulate you in the future.

▶ Learn to meet your own needs – it can be much easier for autism spectrum adults to meet the needs of others than to respect and meet their own needs. Sometimes this is because of alexithymia, which is an inability to recognize emotions (of self and/or others) or a general lack of self-awareness. Manipulators will try to ensure that your needs are never a priority and this can be disastrous in terms of increased meltdowns/shutdowns and anxiety as well as depression.

▶ Do not accept blame for other people's behaviour – you can only be responsible for your own behaviour and the way that you respond to other people. If you do not accept blame, you will not feel guilty for things that are not your fault. This sort of guilt is also very damaging to your sense of self and to the health of your relationships with others.

▶ Be kind and considerate to others but firm about what you are willing and not willing to do for others – if you are known not to give in to pressure then people are less likely to try to manipulate you.

▶ Learn to compromise in areas of a relationship that you can compromise in happily; for example, going to a partner's family home for a meal occasionally because it makes them happy even though you do not enjoy it much. Compromise does not involve guilt, shame or blame, or only one person, both/all people should compromise at times.

If there are children or other vulnerable people involved in the household, it is very important to end a manipulative relationship as soon as possible. This is because manipulation often becomes worse and worse and is a core aspect of an abusive relationship. Children who see abuse suffer emotionally in the short and long term, even if they themselves are not victims of any abuse.

You or your partner are abusive to each other

When people think of domestic/family violence they often wonder why the victim doesn't just leave the perpetrator. Domestic violence is often something that develops slowly rather than appearing as soon as two people meet. Due to the difficulties in social communication experienced by autism spectrum adults, it can be even more difficult for them to know if their partner is being abusive. Abusive relationships include those in which one of the people is paid to support or care for the other, as well as relationships where people live together without payment taking place.

Abuse in adult relationships can be:

- physical

- sexual

- emotional

- only in private

- in public (in front of other people)

- any combination of some/all of the above.

All genders can be victims or perpetrators of abuse, it is not just men who abuse and women who are victims. Children who hear/see domestic violence can be seriously affected, even if they are not personally targeted. For these children the effects have been demonstrated to change their brains as well as impact on their life outcomes negatively (Stien and Kendall 2014). Domestic abuse gets worse over time; that is to say, the actions of the abuser become more extreme and the impact on the victim(s) more severe.

Physical abuse

Physical abuse in a relationship results from the action of a person who, with an object or a part of their body, physically makes contact with another person in a way that results in feelings of injury and/or physical pain to any body part of the victim. Often the person who commits the physical abuse will say they are sorry, or that it was because things got out of control, or because in their opinion the victim 'asked for it'. Physical abuse often starts off small, say with a slap occasionally or a push/shove.

> Lynne: I had really good sex and relationship education at school and they said 'if a man hits you once, leave, because they will do it again and again and again if you don't'. But I was a lesbian and I assumed that they meant women wouldn't hurt other people, so I wouldn't need to worry about this. Years later when I was living with a girlfriend and she hit me when we were having an argument, I believed her when she later said she was sorry, she had just got carried away. The next excuse she used was that it was my fault – I provoked her into hitting me. Within six months she was regularly hurting me and I truly believed it was my fault. When my college tutor asked me if everything was OK because she had noticed some of my bruises, I said I was fine. I don't know why I did this, probably because we are taught to say fine when we are growing up, so we don't ever

think that people really want to know. My girlfriend started to threaten to cut me with a knife and then I got scared, really scared, but I didn't know what to do, where to go, how to handle it. It seemed easier to just get drunk a lot. Then I didn't notice so much. Luckily for me, she got bored of me and threw me out into the street with a plastic shopping bag of my clothes. I was an alcoholic mess, but at least she hadn't killed me.

Physical abuse can be any of the following:

▶ biting

▶ choking

▶ denial of food

▶ forced feeding

▶ kicking

▶ physical restraint

▶ punching

▶ pushing or shoving

▶ scratching

▶ slapping

▶ strangling

▶ threats of violence

▶ throwing things

▶ use of weapons.

None of these are OK, ever, no matter who does these to you. In some relationships there is an element of consensual restraint, slapping or biting during sex, particularly where the relationship is based on sadomasochism or bondage and domination. However, if this is the case it is still *not* OK for this to move out of the sexual arena and into everyday activities. See Chapter 17 for further details.

If you find that you have done or do some of the above when angry or frustrated, you must seek help from a counsellor/ therapist/psychologist or psychiatrist. Your family doctor may also be able to suggest where you can get some help to manage your anger safely. There are a number of programmes run by people who used to be violent to their partners and/or children who are no longer violent. These programmes offer a safe space to come to terms with your behaviour and the effects on people around you, and provide mentoring for you to become a better person.

If you have any kind of relationship with someone who does any of the above to you, it is imperative that you leave them. However, you need to be aware that leaving a violent person can place you (and any children you have) at significant risk. For this reason it is important to get help from a local refuge or centre to manage how to leave safely. Women's refuges can also help men who want to leave violent/abusive relationships. It is a good idea to call the police and an ambulance if you are injured by a partner. In most countries there are laws in place to protect victims of domestic violence and, although you may be fearful of the consequences of involving the police, the consequences of not doing so can be equally bad or even worse.

Do not believe that the violence against you is your fault, it is not. Burning dinner, accidentally breaking a glass, forgetting to buy milk and other everyday things that go wrong are *not* reasons for someone to physically hurt someone else. There is also no justification to use violence because someone says something the person does not like. People who say it is your fault that they are hurting you do *not* love you – they just want to control and manipulate you.

Sexual abuse

Sexual abuse in a relationship is where the perpetrator forces the victim to engage in sexual activity that they do not want to engage in. This may be sexual assault/rape by the partner or being made to engage in sexual activity with other people for their pleasure when you do not want to. A partner or spouse does not have the right to have sex with you whenever they want: all sex, even within a relationship must be consensual to be legal in most countries. However, there are a few countries that do not recognize rape within marriage as rape.

Sexual violence can be committed by anyone and anyone can be a victim. It can happen within any kind of relationship and is rarely about sex, but usually about power. The aggressor enjoys asserting their power and making the victim feel powerless and/or helpless.

> Ann: My partner wanted to have sex how he wanted it, regardless of what I wanted and it didn't matter if I said no or if I cried, he just went right ahead. I don't know why I didn't go and get help, I guess I just believed him that because I lived with him in his house that he had the right to do what he wanted with my body. Then he brought some friends home and they got drunk and he wanted me to let them all have sex with me. I just freaked out and ran away. I went down the street to the phone box and called my dad. He came and got me and I moved home for a while. I think that I should have left the first time he didn't listen to me saying no and just went ahead. It wasn't nice and it has put me off sex. I don't much like to be around men now by myself and so I don't really go out at night. My dad has got me an appointment with a counsellor, because he says I can get my confidence back, it will just take time. I hope so.

Partners who force sexual activity through threats and/or actual violence do not love you, they are just using you and you should contact a support service such as women's refuge or a local community centre to access help to leave safely. Victims of sexual abuse within relationships can feel a sense of shame and try to hide what is happening, but it is not their fault and it is important to seek help as soon as possible to minimize the emotional and/or physical harm that can occur.

If you have forced or tried to force a partner into sexual activity that they do not want to engage in, this is *not* OK. You do not have the right to impose your sexual ideas or desires on anyone else. This is the case even if you are paying a sex worker to have sex with you. The sex worker still has a right to say no. If you have been or are being sexually abusive to someone because you did not realize that it was wrong, you still need to stop *now* and seek help from a therapist to ensure that it does not happen again. Not only is it illegal, so you could be arrested and imprisoned, it is also a terrible thing to do to someone.

In addition to possibly being imprisoned you may be given a court order that forbids you to contact or be within a certain number of metres/feet of your victim, whether you are charged with physical or sexual assault. If you are found guilty of a sexual offence, you may also be listed on a sexual offenders register, which will render you unable to live near a school or playground and unable to do a large number of jobs. You will be stigmatized and hated by the majority of society. It is possible to stop behaving in this abusive way with a skilled therapist over time, so it is important to get assistance to change as soon as possible.

Emotional abuse

Emotional abuse can also be committed by and experienced by anyone in any type of relationship. This type of abuse can be just as traumatic as physical and sexual violence, as the emotional abuse can destroy confidence and self-esteem in the victim. It can be hard to work out if you are being emotionally abused, especially if you have been told all your life that you misinterpret and misunderstand people because you are autistic. Again it is nothing to be ashamed of if you are a victim and it is *not* your fault, no matter what the perpetrator says.

Signs that might indicate that you are in an emotionally abusive relationship are that you:

▶ are afraid of your partner

▶ are called names or ridiculed or humiliated by your partner

▶ are constantly afraid of your partner leaving you as you feel completely dependent on them

▶ feel intimidated or threatened by your partner

▶ feel like you are never good enough for your partner

▶ feel like you are going crazy, or feel confused about the truth.

Behaviours that are emotionally abusive include:

▶ being possessive or controlling of someone – thinking that they belong to you and you can control what they do, when they do it and even how they do it, including things like telling people what to wear and when

▶ belittling someone by name calling, public embarrassment and/or blaming them for everything

- ▶ bullying by deliberately and repeatedly saying/doing hurtful things to someone

- ▶ causing someone to feel afraid, intimidated or threatened

- ▶ controlling someone's money or preventing someone from working or stealing/taking money from them to ensure their financial dependence on you

- ▶ isolating someone by limiting their freedom of movement and/or stopping someone from contacting their friends or family, whether due to jealousy or just to be controlling

- ▶ pretending not to notice someone's presence, conversation or value so that they feel rejected and/or humiliated

- ▶ yelling, insulting or swearing at someone repeatedly.

These behaviours are designed to destroy someone's self-esteem and confidence over a period of time, Sometimes the person behaving like this consciously knows this, while other people are simply repeating patterns of behaviour that they think are OK or normal. Whatever the reason someone behaves in an emotionally abusive way, it is *not* OK. If you are in an emotionally abusive relationship, the abuse is likely to get worse over time and it important to seek help to leave safely.

If you do any of the emotionally abusive behaviour listed above, you need to accept that this is *not* OK and that you need to stop behaving in this way. Emotional abuse is not loving someone or caring for or about them. It is destructive and unhealthy for all concerned. Emotional abuse can also have a significant impact on the mental health of both the abuser and victim.

One of the reasons that it can be very difficult to end an abusive relationship is that the abusive relationship may not be violent or abusive all the time. The person who is abusive may appear to be very kind, caring and loving at other times and apologize for their abusive behaviour. This contradictory behaviour can make it hard for the victim to accept that they are a victim of domestic/family abuse, and can even make it difficult for them to stay angry and upset with the perpetrator. However, the probability of the abusive behaviour continuing and getting worse over time is very high. Abusive people can often appear very nice to other people. They are often being nice in order to manipulate other people's view of them and try to make sure that no one believes you about their abuse.

If you are thinking that you might be in an abusive relationship from reading this section, it can help you to note down things that happen to you, so that you can stop feeling confused about the truth or believing that you are going crazy or are at fault for everything. Once you accept that your relationship is abusive, you need a plan to leave. Sadly, people who are trying to, or who have just left abusive relationships are at a very real risk of being seriously physically injured or even killed by their abuser. It seems that some abusers think that if 'I can't have you, no one can'. For this reason, it is always a good idea to seek out support from others to help you to leave as safely as possible.

If you live in a country where there are women's refuges or domestic violence shelters, these are good places to start to ask for help. These services will support anyone trying to escape domestic/family violence/abuse and are free and confidential. Some services offer free accommodation in a safe house while they help you to sort things out.

I think it is worthwhile to understand that it is better for your mental and physical health to be alone and even lonely than it is to be in an abusive relationship. No-one is so important or amazing that they have a right to hurt you physically, sexually and/or emotionally. In a good relationship, there is a fairly even balance of power and no one is controlled by someone else. Asking someone to do something is OK, telling them to do it is not, especially when it is something that you want for your own pleasure or fun and they do not like or want to do that thing.

> Lisa: My ex used to tell me what to wear every day and, if we went out, what I had to put on. Initially I was fine with that because I know the world judges us on what we wear and I really have no sense of what looks OK and what doesn't. I am only interested if it is comfortable or not. But then he started to buy me new clothes and threw out my favourite clothes saying I looked like a pig in them. He even picked my underwear and it was really awful where the underwires dug into me and the bit on the bottoms went up my bum. I hated it, but he said I looked sexy and he really liked it, so I kinda figured it must be OK. But it just didn't stop, I couldn't pick anything and if I did he got really angry and kept telling me how stupid I was and everyone would think I was really ugly if I went out wearing those shoes or that top. He even took me to the hairdresser to say how I had to cut my hair. I cried and cried when I saw my new haircut, I didn't look like me anymore. I didn't understand if he didn't like anything about the way I looked, why did he want to be in a relationship with me? It made me feel so sad. Now, just putting on my soft clothes that don't squish me or go up my bum, oh it makes me feel good, like happy that I can be me. I am happy living alone, though I do have a boyfriend now. He has to prove he likes me for who I am before I will ever live with him though. I think I might wear slippers to our next date and see what he says!

References

Stien, P. and Kendall, J.C. (2014) *Psychological Trauma and the Developing Brain: Neurologically Based Interventions for Troubled Children.* London: Routledge.

14

Maintaining Long-Term Relationships

Movies are not very good examples to try to understand how to maintain a long-term relationship. For a start they often depict perfect relationships, or relationships that end fatally. Most people in long-term relationships choose to live together, and, if you do, this is hard work initially but also requires long-term effort on both sides to make the relationship work. If there are more than two adults (polyamory) involved in the relationship this makes it even more complicated. See Chapter 18 for information about how children affect relationships.

Some people in long-term relationships prefer to maintain separate space, whether that is in a shared house or two separate homes. Of course living apart means that you cannot split the rent/mortgage and so costs more, but for some people it works well. However, just because you think you may live with someone long term does not mean that you will automatically split the household costs. Each couple will need to work out their own preference for finances, where to live and how to be around each other in public and in private.

Many couples do not discuss money in depth prior to moving into a property together and this can lead to a lot of complications within the relationship. It is not vital to have the same attitude to money but it really helps. For example, if you do not like to buy things on credit or get into debt and your future live-in partner has four credit cards that are all up to the limit (known as maxed out), it is likely that you will have friction about money at some point.

If you choose to live in separate homes then usually you are each responsible for your own bills and keep all your own income (unless children are involved). If someone you start to date begins asking for money from you this is a warning sign that things might not be safe in the long term. There are people who go out with those who cannot read social and/or emotional cues very well in order to extract money from them. These people *never* love you; they are using you for their own financial gain.

Likewise, if you live with someone and are asked to give them all your money, this is not a good idea as it leaves you vulnerable and financially dependent. Having joint bank accounts is normal in a long-term relationship but more and more people are only putting part of their income into the joint account and keeping some for themselves in their own bank account. Even if you are both dependent on welfare it is a good idea to ensure you have some money saved for yourself in case things go wrong and you need to find yourself a place to live by yourself or with your children.

Attitudes to money generally fall into the types depicted in Table 14.1:

Table 14.1 Attitudes to money

Thrifty (sometimes known as stingy or tight)	Careful (sometimes known as risk averse)	Generous	Wasteful (said to spend money like there is no tomorrow or that money burns a hole in their pocket)
Will save money as much as possible.

Will shop for bargains and only buy what is necessary.

Will never buy on credit (buying on tick or hire purchase) except for buying a home.

May not have credit cards; if they do they will pay the balance in full every month.

Will recycle and reuse items whenever possible (make do and mend). | Will save some money and have some for buying things they want but do not need.

May buy on credit where there is no interest to pay.

Will shop for bargains but also buy full price items.

Balances possible future financial needs against current desires to spend, pays bills before spending on luxuries. | Often buys gifts and things for others.

Like to spend money on other people.

Not bothered if things are not on special, but will buy bargains if they are 'a good deal'.

Happy to buy things on credit if they think it will make them or someone else happy.

Happy to pay their share of household bills but may need reminding.

Will often save if asked to contribute to a savings account by a spouse/long-term partner. | Spends their income very quickly on things that they feel like buying whether or not they need them.

May gamble their money.

Buys things that are too expensive.

Enjoys spending money.

May not have enough money left to pay their share of household bills.

Doesn't usually save.

May not notice bills and may not make any attempt to pay them. |

Clearly, being wasteful is irresponsible and, if you are thrifty or careful, it would be very stressful to be involved in a living together relationship with someone wasteful. Some generous people can find careful or thrifty people equally frustrating and stressful. It is important to not only understand what kind of financial attitude your future partner may have but how you would organize your personal and joint finances. This is generally not something that you discuss on your first date or when you first meet someone as this information is very personal and not usually shared by people who are not very good friends or in a relationship. There are various ways to organize your finances (Table 14.2).

Trust, honest but caring communication, kindness and an ability to compromise and/or accept things are vital to healthy long-term relationships. Most relationships have conflict at one time or another, but it is how you deal with the conflict that affects how long and successful your relationship is. Without trust in each other, many things that should be fine in a good relationship can become really problematic.

Trust

Trust is a concept that encompasses a whole set of beliefs and attitudes and these require building up rather than being there at the very start of a relationship before you have got to know each other. When you develop confidence and faith in your partner that they are honest with you, have integrity and loyalty, and that they respect you, this forms the basis of trust in a relationship. If you trust each other you would reasonably expect your partner to keep their promises to you as well as to stay with you and work on the relationship when things are not as good between you, for whatever reason.

Table 14.2 Ways to organize money

Completely separate	Mostly separate but a household bills account is joint	Mostly shared money but with separate accounts for each partner as well	All shared
Each person pays part of the bills and when the couple go out each person pays their own share (going Dutch). In this case it may help to have a written agreement about exactly how the bills will be split (e.g. 50% each or X will pay the power but Z will pay the phone, etc.).	Each person pays a pre-agreed amount into the household bills account. This account may be used for all joint expenses or just bills/rent/mortgage. In some couples the amount paid is a % of each person's income (e.g. 60% or for others it might be a fixed amount, say $200 a week).	Each person keeps some of their own income to use how they want. The shared money will pay for all joint activities as well as some things that are not done together. This varies between couples.	All income is pooled into one shared account. Each person can spend from the account. It is important to be aware that some people lie about this situation and do hide some of their own money. This is not always for a negative reason but it can be.

Autistic spectrum adults can hold on to past experiences forever and assume that if one person has treated them in a particular way that this will always happen or that everyone will do that. A person's past experiences and emotions create expectations about each new relationship, and these expectations can be helpful or damaging. If you find it very hard to trust because of prior life experiences, it may help your current relationship to work on these trust issues together, or by yourself with a therapist, as a lack of trust can be very damaging.

When people within a relationship disclose private/personal events, attitudes or feelings, these should be respected and kept in confidence and not talked about with others. Talking about a partner's private issues can break down trust. Another thing that can break down trust is having a sexual relationship with someone outside the relationship, when you have agreed to be faithful/monogamous/not to have sex with others. Addiction issues within a relationship can erode trust as the addict tries to hide or lie about things to cover up their addiction.

To build trust, the people in the relationship should communicate openly and honestly but with kindness. So, for example, it would be more helpful to say, 'Please could you clean your teeth before we kiss as it is nicer for me then?' and less helpful to say 'Your breath stinks, I am not kissing you.' If you are in a relationship with someone who is not on the autism spectrum, they may well have a very different idea about open communication and may find your honesty too blunt and hurtful at times. It is important to negotiate these communication issues and work out a way that you can both understand each other better.

Communication

Communication is the two-way exchange of information so that both/all people gain a shared understanding of what is being communicated. For those who are on the autism spectrum this two-way exchange can be problematic. In part, these problems arise because of the different way autistics and non-autistics use words. Typical people use words within a social context, whereas autistics tend to use words to convey information factually. This is not a minor difference and can lead to both/ all people in the relationship believing that 'something' has been effectively communicated, when in fact they each have a different understanding of what that 'something' is and what it means for all concerned.

Not only do typical people use words with a social context, they also rely heavily on contextual clues such as tone of voice, facial expression and other body language. These types of clues are rarely used by autistics, who can also use atypical body language as well as misread that of others. The way that many people on the autism spectrum move their bodies or body parts to express their emotions is individual and not well understood by the general public. For example, if you flap to show that you are happy, and pace when anxious, you may need to explicitly explain this to friends or to people with whom you are in a relationship.

In turn you may also need to ask them to explain their emotional expressions and what sort of reaction they want and do not want from you. You may or may not be able to react in the ways that your partner would like, but you can at least try to avoid reacting in ways that they do not want. For example, if your girlfriend says that she cries when she hears sad songs and that she does not want you to ask her what is wrong, then it is a good idea to not ask her what is wrong if you notice her crying when she is listening to music. However, if she is crying and there is no music on, then you may want to ask her what is wrong.

One of the basics of communication in a relationship is honesty; however, honesty in a social context can be different from an autistic version of honesty. As you get to know someone, whether as a friend, colleague or in a sexual relationship, you need to explore this issue of honest communication:

- ▶ How much information do you each want in response to a question?

- ▶ Are there times when honesty is not the best policy? What are these and why?

- ▶ If information is left out/left unsaid is that seen as lying or seen as not important? How can you know which?

- ▶ How can you communicate in a way that is respectful but that still conveys your needs and wants?

- ▶ How can you express support for and care about each other?

- ▶ When are you going to discuss major issues? How are you going to do this?

- ▶ If you get angry or have a disagreement are there any particular triggers for meltdowns? How are you going to manage your/their meltdowns and still find a way forward through the disagreement?

- ▶ Are you expected to be less open/honest/communicative with each other's families or friends, or is this not an issue?

- ▶ How are you going to ensure levels of emotional and/or sexual intimacy that are respectful and a balance between people's needs/desires for time alone/together?

A lack of effective communication can lead not just to misunderstandings but also mistrust, tension, defensiveness, frustration and even anger, all of which can magnify any possible issues and lead to more intense conflict. Many autistics abhor conflict and can lie or otherwise to try to avoid conflict; however, conflict is a healthy and normal part of a long-term relationship. It can be useful to find a strategy that works in your relationship for everyone, where conflict resolution takes place in a safe and meaningful way while avoiding any triggers for meltdowns.

> Lucy: I seem quite verbal and I wasn't diagnosed until middle age, but looking back it was clear my literal understanding of language and my total lack of understanding of the social context led to most of the problems in my relationships. If my partner would ask if they looked good in a particular outfit, I would answer honestly, even when they told me they just bought it especially or it was a gift from their mum or something. It wasn't until I met other autistic adults in my late middle age and heard their explanations about the way typical people communicate, that I understood I had spent years offending a series of partners because I did not get tact!

> Sam: My girlfriend had a hysterectomy, which meant she had to go to hospital for a few days. I was totally freaked out because she wanted me to visit her and everything would be unpredictable until she was home and feeling better. She listened to me for a few minutes, then quietly and calmly said; 'It is not all about you, love. I am the one having surgery and it is scary for me too. Let's talk about how it is for both of us and what we can do to get through it.' She wasn't angry with me because she knows how my Asperger's can make me see the world from my perspective a lot. A few years ago I would have got all angry if someone said something like that to me, but now I just try to listen, she is really good at helping me understand what she needs in order to feel loved and valued and then I can try to do these things. After all she tries hard to communicate with me in ways I understand and in ways that help me.

> Mike: My boyfriend hadn't told his parents he was gay and he wanted me to pretend I was his flatmate when his family came to visit. I got really angry with him and had to go and shut myself in the bedroom each time he brought it up. It was getting

so bad I thought we would break up. Then one of my friends suggested I text him if I couldn't actually talk about it without getting angry and to text and ask him why he didn't want his family to know. This friend is in a relationship with another aspie and they SMS each other all the time because they can process it easier, although sometimes they still misunderstand each other. I think relationships just are hard work no matter who you are.

It can be hard for anyone to apologize to someone, but part of being in a relationship is valuing the other person enough to say sorry when you do or say something that upsets them or makes them feel unloved or unvalued. It is also right to acknowledge when you are wrong and they are right, even if you only work this out days or even weeks later. The other side of apologizing is forgiving, and this is a necessary part of a long-term relationship too (unless your partner is abusive, in which case, see Chapter 13).

Kindness

One of the ways long-term relationships thrive is through the expression of kindness by the people within that relationship. Kindness is a way to demonstrate love, care and liking for a person. Kindness is often explained as being generous in spirt, caring, acting in an ethical way, being considerate and thoughtful. It is seen as a virtue in many faiths and, in the 4th century BC, Aristotle is said to have defined kindness as 'helpfulness towards someone in need, not in return for anything, nor for the advantage of the helper himself, but for that of the person helped'. Nowadays this is seen as defining altruism, of which kindness is often a part.

Being kind requires an attention to the needs of others that may not be an intrinsic quality of people on the autism spectrum; however, this can be learnt as can many actions which others interpret as kindness or thoughtfulness. However, being kind can enhance a sense of wellbeing for everyone involved, and many acts of kindness are completely free and easy to implement. Kindness is expressed in different ways by different people.

Planned acts of kindness can appear to be a bit stilted or contrived, but they are helpful as practice and in order to hardwire the brain pathways into becoming more conscious of kindness and enable kindness to become habitual. As you become kinder and express your kindness more frequently, both you and the recipients of your kindness (your partner(s)) benefit. Trust can be built and reinforced with kindness, and kindness can act as a relationship lifeboat in times of distress, enabling the relationship to float along until you are all able to address the issues that need addressing.

Acts of kindness in a relationship include things like:

- saying yes when your partner asks you to do something for them

- spontaneously doing one of your partner's household chores for them

- making your partner a drink and/or meal before/after work

- smiling at your partner and telling them that you love them

- praising and appreciating your partner

- helping your partner with things they struggle with and letting them help you with things you struggle with

- making time to spend together

- making time for your partner to have some time to do something they really want to do

- picking some flowers and giving them to your partner

- listening to your partner if they want to talk

- asking your partner what you can do to help if they are sad/angry/stressed/frustrated, and then doing what they asked you to do

- asking your partner if they want to come and look at the beautiful sunset/sunrise/stars/moon with you

- always saying something kind or positive to your partner before you go to sleep and when you first wake up, even if all you say is 'I love you'.

Lucy: I like to go to bed early and my girlfriend likes to stay up really late watching TV. I hate sound or noise in the bedroom when I am trying to sleep and so she has to watch TV in another room. I get up much earlier in the morning than her as I have to commute to work and she works from home. Sometimes, it gets me really frustrated that her TV is disturbing my sleep but then I remind myself that my getting up early disturbs her sleep and that if we are both considerate and kind then we will both be disturbed less and so feel less grumpy!

John: My partner asks me for a goodnight hug every night and gives me a quick kiss on my forehead as I hate lip to lip kissing. Then he says, 'love you, goodnight' and goes to sleep. In the morning, I wake up as he is kissing my forehead really gently and it is so gentle and lovely, then we both say 'good morning, I love you' before getting up. They are such little things but so reassuring and comforting. I think that it is a big part of why we are till happy together after eight years.

In a long-term relationship everyone needs to be kind not just to each other but also to themselves. This requires self-acceptance and acceptance of each other.

Acceptance and compromise

Long-term relationships need to be worked on as people change over the years – different things may become easier and/or more difficult in the relationship. This is normal and happens in most relationships. Sexual activity within a relationship often decreases dramatically within long-term relationships after the first few years, and this can impact people within the relationship differently. How people within a relationship deal with their particular issues will be unique to them; however, all relationships require acceptance and fair compromise in order to succeed long term.

It is not fair, equitable or healthy for one person in the relationship to do all the compromising. Unfair compromising is where one person gives up the things that they want or feel they need for a healthy relationship and the other person does not. Balance is important in a relationship, in terms of compromise and power. All the people in a relationship should share power so that no one is disproportionately more important than anyone else, and compromise should also be shared to prevent resentment and anger building up, which can destroy trust and hinder kindness.

Acceptance needs to be of self and other, so that you can accept yourselves and each other. Also, you should not confuse support needs with dependence, as healthy relationships are made up of independent people who may or may not have some/all of their support needs met by their partner. No one should be dependent on their partner: they should be able to think for themselves and be free to express themselves within their relationship and in the wider world.

One of the things that can be hard for partners to accept about each other is the other person's interests and/or friends. For example, if your partner wants to watch football every weekend with their friends at your house, this may really irritate you. You can deal with this in a number of ways: by getting cross, by being rude to his friends and hoping they never come back, by asking if all the friends can take turns hosting the group so they are only at your house once a month or less, by going out somewhere when his friends are over, etc. Some of these ideas will create conflict, while others will demonstrate support for your partner and his interests. Some ask for compromise on both sides, while some are a compromise on one side only. If you rarely or never compromise, it is reasonable to assume that your partner should never have to compromise either!

However, there are useful and healthy compromises and there are unhealthy compromises. Unhealthy compromises involve one person giving up things they like/want or need in order to fulfill a request by their partner. This is closely linked to emotional abuse (see Chapter 13) and will end up with the person who gives things up feeling resentful and/or unloved and unvalued – which would be true. However, some people give up things because they assume that doing so will make their partner happy and/or impress them and they are doing so to 'look/seem good'. This can be described as being a martyr, which is something that seems to be common to many people who feel insecure in their relationship.

Unhealthy compromises involve changing or giving up something inherent to yourself, such as not flapping or twirling in your home. Even if your flapping or twirling makes you look different to typical people, this is not a reason to stop yourself from expressing your emotions at home in this way.

Your home is your safe space and sanctuary and you shouldn't give up or compromise on such fundamentals as authentic self-expression. A compromise might be that you try not to flap or twirl at your partner's work event, but that your partner agrees that you can leave after only 30–45 minutes at the event.

Healthy compromises are about both trying to grow and develop together in ways that help you to achieve your individual potentials, as well as succeed as a couple. This involves each person learning to understand, accept and value themselves as well as learning to understand, accept and value their partner in a supportive, kind, considerate and caring way.

> Bec: My partner has got really good at telling me when she needs me to just listen and be supportive by saying things like, 'that must be really stressful', or 'that sounds awful' instead of doing what I normally want to do, which is give an unwanted lecture on all the other ways the situation could be dealt with. In turn I have learnt to compromise by accepting that we are different people and just because doing something my way is right for me, does not mean it is right for her. In telling her what she should have done, I wasn't validating her or demonstrating my care and love for her. As an aspie I have really struggled to accept that my way is not the only way or even the only right way, but as a couple we are much happier because of this compromise and I am still me and she is still herself too.

Even things like housework and other chores need to be worked out, and acceptance and healthy compromise can be very helpful in these day-to-day areas of a relationship. Where one person has less energy than the other, no matter what the reason, a compromise might be reached where the chores are not evenly divided, but divided according to how manageable they are for each person. Other compromises might be around the type of food bought and how it is cooked and served.

Lynne: I hate junk food, even though it seems all the other aspies I know love junk food, I hate the smell of it all. I like fresh food, made into something hot by me (or someone else). My partner could live on roast chicken, but I don't like the bones – yuck! So our compromise is that even though I can get really tired and overwhelmed, I get to shop and cook all the time, but that if my partner does cook for me, I have to stay out of the kitchen and I have to not complain about it! It works for us, but it took a while to work this out. Before, I used to get all control freak about the kitchen and would hover around upsetting her with my critical instructions about how to cook stuff properly.

If you really hate confrontation, you may find yourself compromising all the time in order to avoid any conflict, but this is not a healthy way to have a relationship. It may be that you can work out a system to express your wants and needs in a non-confrontational way, such as emailing, texting, drawing or leaving post-it notes for your partner. Relationships are made up of two or more adults, and should be on the basis that the people involved are viewed as equally important in the relationship. If you compromise too much, you may be making your partner very uncomfortable or implying that you do not value yourself in the relationship.

You should accept each other's right to say no to any type of sexual activity as well as to dress in any way that is legal, and to have friends of your own choosing. Acceptance of each other's careers/jobs or study or voluntary work is also important, as these can be a part of someone's identity. Even if one or both of you needs to move work/study places in order to make your relationship work, there should be acceptance and support for the work/study and how to continue this so you can both achieve what you want to.

Many adults on the autism spectrum require a significant amount of 'me time' within a relationship, and it is useful to let people know this before you live together if you are hoping to make your relationship work long term. Some people choose to live separately or to have separate bedrooms, and these choices support their long-term relationships. For other people the idea of having separate bedrooms would be so distressing that it could end a relationship. If you are still learning to understand the way you experience and express your autism/ Asperger's, then it can help your partner if you are clear about any sensory issues and you find solutions and strategies to support you both to live well together, even if this means some compromise.

> Jo: I am really noise sensitive and I hate the TV ads because they come on louder and, even though I know it is going to happen, it just enrages me. If I am home by myself, I listen to the TV really quietly, but if my wife is home, she has it on quite loud, though the volume indicator is only about 40%. She wanted me to buy some noise cancelling headphones, but I didn't want to because I thought I would look silly. After a few years of me taking the remote and turning it down and her taking it back and turning it up, I got some headphones and they are awesome! I can't even hear the washing machine if I put the noise cancelling on. I don't know why I didn't try her suggestion a few years ago – we could have saved ourselves a lot of stress.

15

Sexual Activity and Sexual Pleasure

Sexual activity is any action that gives a person sexual pleasure. For example, when someone eats an apple, it may be pleasurable but not in a sexual way. Their body does not have any physical reactions in terms of sexual excitement such as increased blood flow to the genitals, increase in heart rate, dilation of pupils, tingling in body parts. However, when that same someone kisses their partner they may well have some or all of those physical expressions of sexual excitement. For men or others with a penis, increased blood flow to the penis results in the penis swelling and holding itself up and away from the body. This is known as an erection. The clitoris on women swells with increased blood flow and becomes more sensitive, which can be pleasurable for some people and painful for others. Sexual excitement is also signalled by the vagina becoming lubricated from the inside.

People can engage in sexual activity, whether by themselves or with another person/people in a variety of places. However, in most places it is illegal to engage in any form of sexual activity in a public place and, if you are caught, you can be arrested and charged with public indecency. In some countries the penalties are much harsher than other countries. People who do engage in sexual activities outside, need to ensure that they are not able to be seen by other people to avoid breaking the law.

Sexual activities are deemed inherently private in most cultures, which is at odds with the way female bodies are sexualized and used as marketing tools in many cultures. For example, women in bikinis may be used to help sell cars at a car show. The marketing implication being that if you buy this car, you may attract this kind of woman. In addition, pornography is freely and easily accessible to most people via the internet. Some available pornography is illegal, such as that involving animals and/or children, while some is produced by exploiting people, usually women.

Some pornography is self-created and sold online by entrepreneurs, often in a subscription model. It may be that you explore pornography because you are interested in understanding what sorts of sexual activities are possible or to see particular types of sex. However, what is depicted in pornography is rarely typical or even possible for most people. Research has indicated that habitual viewing of pornography can damage the real sexual relationships of people over time. In addition, some people can become addicted to pornography and this can substitute for or replace real relationships. If pornography begins to affect your mood, sleep, daily functioning and/or relationships, you should seek professional help to break the addiction. Treatment can take the form of out-patient or in-patient therapy.

However, occasional viewing of pornography to elicit a sexual response in yourself and/or your partner should

SEXUAL ACTIVITY AND SEXUAL PLEASURE

not be problematic. Pornography can be visual, written or aural. Couples should be able to discuss their opinions of pornography openly and decide what role, if any, it will have in a long-term relationship.

> Laura: When I was at high school the boys would be giggling and passing around these books and magazines, so I asked to look. One of the boys gave me The Happy Hooker by Xaviera Hollander to read and I just enjoyed it, so when I had finished I took it back and asked if he had another book I could read. The whole time I was friends with this boy (though now I look back I realize we were not friends, he copied my homework and I let him, and in exchange he loaned me his porn collection to read. I used to masturbate while reading and I still like written porn. Videos or porn movies don't excite me at all because I don't find conventional beauty sexually attractive – I like curvy women with real women type bodies. I don't mind if I am single because I can give myself an orgasm. If I am in a relationship I have found that my partners don't tend to like me reading porn around them. They have told me that I shouldn't need porn, that they should be enough, but it is nothing to do with that for me, I just like reading it and imagining me within it. I like them and sex with them too. So now I hide the porn books in the back of my closet if I am in a relationship.

> Jill: My husband was addicted to porn on the internet. It was terrible – the more he watched, the more weird things he would want me to try. When I said no, he got even more into his internet porn, but it was taking up all his time in the evening and weekends. He wanted us to have orgies at the house and I don't even like being around other people much, let alone having lots of naked people in our house all wanting to have sex with each other everywhere! I googled porn addiction and found that it was a real thing, though I had to print out some information and make my husband read it before he would go and get treatment.

Then I found out he had spent thousands of pounds on a new credit card on these pay per view porn sites. I was so upset. His psychologist is working with him and says that after a while I will need to go in with him for some couples therapy. What a waste of money.

16

Sexual Activity by Yourself

When you engage in sexually pleasurable activities to give yourself an orgasm these are broadly described as masturbation. However, there are all sorts of ways to experience sexual pleasure without orgasm and, as with orgasms, these can be explored by yourself or with someone else. For autistics, sensory differences mean that some touch can be experienced very differently to the same touch experienced by others. If you know what kinds of touch and where are the most pleasurable for you, you will be able to guide future sexual partners so that they bring you pleasure rather than causing you to feel uncomfortable or even feel pain.

Sexual activity can be calming or exciting; people have preferences for what they like, when and how. Every individual is quite different and, although pornography will enable you to see what some sexual activity entails, it will not help you work out what you like. To find this out you need to try things out for yourself. You need to be aware that some things that are written about or on film are not safe in reality. For example, it is very dangerous to put a penis in the tube of a vacuum cleaner or to insert sharp/glass/large objects into a vagina.

> Carl: I find that I really like it when my penis is held firmly, with a hand wrapped around it. If I do this I like to move my hand up and down, keeping the hand wrapped around my penis. As I get more and more feelings it is sort of like my body gets all agitated but in a good way and when this starts to happen I like to keep my hand moving with the same intensity but get a bit quicker, sort of like I can't wait to come (have an orgasm) so I need to move towards the goal quicker and quicker. I really like to sleep after I come, though I don't like to get clothes or anything sticky, so for me it is best to wank [masturbate] in the shower and then I can have a quick wash, and after drying off go to bed and have a nice sleep.

> Felicity: I don't like penetrative sex and I am very uncomfortable having other people touch me, although I am OK with it sometimes. By learning what kinds of sex I like, I have been able to share that with my girlfriends and so it makes it much easier as I am not worrying all the time that they might touch me somewhere I don't like or in a way I don't like. By experimenting with what different touches on different parts of my body feel like, which I did when I was in bed by myself, I could be relaxed and at the same time distracted from analysing my day over and over. I figured out that I really really enjoy having my lower abdomen stroked from hip to hip with fingertips and a light, light touch, whereas I don't like a light touch on my thighs at all – it is more tickly but not nice at all. Plus I giggle when things are tickly, which is OK when I am by myself, but when a girlfriend makes me giggly they get all grumpy really quickly and say I am ruining the mood. This way I can be upfront and say don't touch me lightly here and here, but if you do it here it is awesome.

Unless your masturbation is compulsive and interfering with and preventing day-to-day activities, then it is a healthy and fun activity that is completely free. Compulsive masturbation can be treated by psychologists and/or psychiatrists. Knowing what kinds of touch you like can enable you to bring pleasure to yourself and teach a partner how to pleasure you. However, an interesting difference between self-pleasuring and someone else doing exactly the same things to you, is that the actions do not always feel the same when you do them and when someone else does them.

> Carl: Even if I show a guy how I like to come, and they seem to be doing it just like I would, my penis feels different and my body's reactions are also a bit different. If I am really comfortable with the guy and excited to be having sex with them, the feelings and reactions can be even more intense, but if I am not really that interested and just doing it to fill some time, then it is kind of like nice but not really, really nice, if that makes sense.

There are a number of myths around masturbation that have been passed down generations to try to prevent people from masturbating as it was seen as a sin in a number of religions and so these faiths tried to stop the practice. However, it is accepted that there are some health benefits of masturbation – it can relax your muscles, help you to fall asleep, reduce stress and improve self-esteem because orgasm promotes the release of endorphins, which are the brain's opioid-like neurotransmitters that cause feelings of physical and mental wellbeing.

Masturbation does not cause blindness or mental health issues or reduce a person's sexual function. In fact it can improve mental health through the individual feeling more positive after the release of endorphins. Sexual function can be improved through self-discovery and many people who struggle to orgasm with a partner are able to do so by themselves.

Some people find the use of sex toys useful to help them orgasm, or to experience different sensations. Sex toys, such as dildos (pretend penis) and vibrators, should be washed thoroughly between uses and stored in a clean dry place. They should not be shared with others unless completely clean as they can transmit a number of diseases, just as a real penis can. In addition, they can attract dust and dirt if they are not kept in a container/drawer/cupboard.

Examples of sex toys are: dildos, vibrators, butt plugs (dildos for the anus), blow up dolls, benwah/kegel balls, pulsators and prostate massagers. These toys can be made from plastic, latex, rubber or other materials. They often require lubricant to be used safely. Lubricants can be silicone- or water-based, and some lubricants are not safe to use with condoms as they can react with the condom and this can result in sperm being able to leak through.

Some people are allergic to certain lubricants and/or condoms. It is helpful to know this before you are having sex with someone else, as it would be awful to suddenly have a burning or painful sensation and be unsure why!

Sexual activity does not have to be centred around an orgasm: it might be touching your skin or hair in a particular way, for example. Also, the way you touch yourself is unlikely to be the way any partner wants to be touched. Self-pleasure helps you to become familiar with your body and to know what you like, so you can enjoy yourself and teach or show your partner what you like.

17

Sexual Activity with Someone Else

Sexual activity with another person is as varied and personal as masturbation: what feels good for you with one partner may not feel the same with another. Engaging in sexual activity with someone else requires consent from both/all people and relies on everyone involved having some level of sexual interest or desire. In addition, you should be aware of sexual health and personal safety issues. You may also want to use a safe word.

A safe word is an explicit system that people can use whereby each person chooses a word that if it is said during sexual activity, signals a need to stop everything immediately. This is commonly used in the sadomasochistic community (S&M) and the bondage and domination (BD) community. Sometimes, these two are grouped together under the acronym of BDSM. Safe words need to be words that are not normally used in your everyday conversation, so, for example, you might choose dandelion, unless you were a gardener or happen to collect dandelions. Each person reminds the other person(s) of their safe word prior to sexual activity, and it is agreed what will happen when a safe word is said.

Examples of what might happen are:

> John: When I say my safe word, the agreement is that all touching, kissing, or anything else will stop immediately and my partner will give me a blanket to wrap myself up in and then go away and leave me alone for ten minutes. I can get hypersensitive to touch so that a nice touch can suddenly feel really painful, so using a safe word has enabled us to try out sex without the idea freaking me out too much.

> Ash: My partner was raped many years ago and she has PTSD [post-traumatic stress disorder], so we have a safe word system so she can feel safe and loved and valued all the time. If she says her word, I know this means to stop anything except hugging, and to hug her real tight and squeeze until she says she is OK now. Often we can carry on what we were doing before after she feels OK again, but it is up to her. I think it is so awful that some people feel they can do stuff without the other person's consent and this is such a small thing to do to make sure she is OK.

> Nina: I knew this girl who would forget to breathe when she was getting close to having an orgasm. I had to keep telling her to breathe. I would have liked a safe word that meant – I'm stopping until you breathe. I was always worried she would faint or get unconscious and I wouldn't know what to do.

Safe words can be particularly useful for people on the autism spectrum who may need a break from the intensity of physical or emotional feeling during sexual activity. For other autistics it can provide a mechanism to ensure that their consent is respected and help them to feel comfortable and confident in engaging in sexual activity.

Sexual activity is often portrayed as only involving a penis and a vagina, with the penis being inserted into and then repeatedly partially withdrawn from the vagina. However, this is only a very small aspect to sexual activity, which is also referred to as penetrative sex, sex or fucking. All these phrases can be used for any sexual act that involves inserting a penis, finger(s) or other object into a vagina, anus or mouth (sometimes called orifices).

Some people like to self-stimulate/masturbate when they are with another person(s) and this is fine. Other people prefer to experience sexual pleasure and/or orgasm from the touch or actions of someone else. This is fine too. Often sexual encounters start with the two people kissing each other. This may be with lips touching lips, or the lips of one person kissing somewhere on the body of the other person. When people are lip kissing, some people like to have their mouths open and let their tongues touch during the kissing. It is OK to like this or not like it. There are no rules about what you should do apart from having consent from everyone involved and not breaking the law.

Kissing someone's body can be slow or quick, concentrated in one area or moving around to kiss the person over a large part of their body. If someone starts off by kissing you slowly and gently and becomes more intense and/or firmer and/or quicker, this often indicates an increase in sexual desire. If you prefer a particular kind of kissing, once you have realized this you need to let your partner(s) know, so that it is as pleasurable as possible for both of you.

Kissing and touching are sometimes referred to as foreplay, with penetrative sex seen as the sex act/action. But for some people, kissing and/or touching are the only sexual activities they enjoy and they do not engage in penetrative sex. Yet other people do not like kissing and/or touching and only enjoy penetrative sex. It can be very confusing if you do not discuss each other's preferences openly. It is perfectly acceptable to ask someone to kiss/touch you in a different way because you prefer it. If you do this, very rarely the other person will get angry. If they do, this is a strong indicator that they are not interested in your pleasure and are focused on their own pleasure at the expense of yours. In general this is a signal that this person is not going to have a positive or supportive relationship with you.

Touching can be with fingertips, hands, body parts or inanimate objects such as feathers, fabrics, textured objects, etc. It can be very light and gentle through to very firm and strong/hard with a myriad of variations inbetween. You might find that you enjoy or dislike types of touch during sexual activity that during other activities have the opposite effect, or you may find that types of touch you don't like normally are even more horrendous at these times. There is no way to predict this without experimenting first. Having open and honest discussions about what different touches feel like on different parts of your body can help your partner to feel confident around your body as they explore how to have the most positive and pleasurable time with you.

Emotions, physical and mental health states can all affect how you experience sexual activity and how you respond to it, and this is quite normal. For example, desire often decreases when people are very tired or stressed, so if you or your partner is very tired, sexual interactions can seem to be more hard work than pleasurable. Some people find sex is a good strategy for releasing stress and tension and they may enjoy sex more when they are stressed, so again being open and honest about your preferences is important.

Felicity: I met this woman who asked if I wanted to fuck when I was in my early 20s. I met her at a lesbian bar and it was unusual because I never knew when people were interested in me but she was quite blunt and clear so I got that! She was in the country on business and didn't want to take me to her hotel, so we went to my flat. But it was weird – once we were there she kind of took charge and gave instructions like: take your clothes off, lie down. I was young, she was interesting and I really liked sex, so I just went along with it. She then said I couldn't touch her, not at all as she hated being touched but loved touching. That was fine by me, it was a really interesting experience. I suppose it was an advantage to being autistic, I wasn't offended by her bluntness, I appreciated knowing what she meant without having to guess if I had interpreted it right.

There are a wide variety of sexual activities for people to engage in, including some that are categorized in special subareas, such as BDSM. All of these activities should be engaged in with respect for the other person(s). Even though some books and movies might suggest that some relationships are based on ideas of slavery, this is not the case for healthy relationships, even when it appears that one person is in charge. Before engaging in any BDSM activities, you should agree safe words with the people involved.

Bondage is an area of sexual activity that involves restraining someone during sexual activity. Restraint needs to be safe and should not impede breathing in any way. Care needs to be taken around sensory issues and health issues when engaging in bondage – in large cities it is possible to attend courses on how to practise bondage safely. Otherwise, if you are interested, it would be good to read some books or blogs first, to get an understanding of the basics. Never engage in BDSM when you or the other person have taken drugs or drunk alcohol, as misjudgements in these situations can be very dangerous. Bondage can be intense or fun and playful. Just make sure that whenever you're engaging in any type of bondage, you need to be able to get your partner out of any restraint in an emergency. Keep some safety scissors nearby all the time and always monitor your partner's circulation.

Domination is where the dominant sexual partner is 'in charge' of the sexual activity and the other person (people) is submissive and 'submits' to the activity. There may or may not be bondage involved. Although it might sound as if one person is in charge, usually the people involved are acting and playing a game that is designed to heighten the sexual pleasure of everyone concerned. For example, one person may like to be less active and more passive than the other, and if this is acted out through fantasy or talk it could be called domination/submission.

> Kara: I orgasm very easily and my partner finds it fun to try to ensure that I have a really big intense orgasm, as this seems to be something that can really help me to self-regulate and be calmer in our day-to-day life. We often do this by him being more dominant and telling me that I am not allowed to orgasm yet, and me acting more submissive and making my body not orgasm yet. Even though I am an aspie control freak, when we act like this I have the most amazing sexual experiences, so much more intense and worthwhile than just regular sex.

> Mike: I have to be in control of what happens when we have sex: where I am touched, how and how long for. My boyfriend understands this and he knows that if I am in control we will have sex, he will get to have his pleasure and I, mine, but if I am not in control, nothing will happen!

Sadomasochism was first discussed in terms of power and control only, by German psychiatrist Richard von Krafft-Ebing in his 1886 book *Psychopathia Sexualis*. Freud popularized the idea that one person could be both sadist and masochist, which modern SM practitioners call switching. Havelock Ellis explored sadomasochism further in his *Studies in the Psychology of Sex* (1897–1928), and argued that the aspects of sadism and masochism are complementary emotional states. Ellis noted that in sadomasochism pain is concerned only with sexual pleasure, and is not used to inflict cruelty, as implied by Freud. This accords with the views of people involved in sadomasochism, who say that pain should only be inflicted or received in love, not in abuse, and only for the pleasure of both participants. This painful pleasure may a core part of the sexual fulfillment of individuals who enjoy sadomasochism.

Fifty Shades of Grey popularized a very simplified and unrealistic version of BDSM, which has more in common with fantasy than reality. However, as long as you are only involved in legal, consenting sexual activity, it is OK to explore your interpretations of any/all aspects of BDSM.

If you want to experiment with a different type of sexual activity but are not sure and your partner is not sure, you should talk about it first. Why do you want to try it? What are you hoping to experience? What are the issues? How will it affect either/both of you from an emotional/physical/sensory perspective?

As with all relationship issues, seeking out and trying various solutions is far more practical and useful than assigning blame or fault. Sex should be fun, it should help create bonds of trust and/or care/love, and it should not cause problems. If it is causing problems, try to address these, whether by yourselves or through relationship counselling.

If you or your sexual partner(s) have any additional health issues or disabilities, this does not mean that you cannot or should not have a healthy sex life. The activities that you may be able to engage in may be restricted or need to be adapted, and the way you/they can bring yourselves/each other pleasure may need to be explored for a while before you find mutually pleasurable activities.

References

Havelock, E. (1897–1928) *Studies in the Psychology of Sex* (Vols. 1–6). Philadelphia, PA: F. A. Davis Co.

Krafft-Ebing, R. (1886) *Psychopathia Sexualis Eine klinisch-forensische Studie*. Stuttgart: Ferdinand Enke.

18

Having Children (Your Own or Other's) and How This Affects Relationships

You may have your own children or acquire someone else's when you start a relationship with someone who already has children. Children of any age can impact on a relationship because of their support needs. Children require adult support for food, clothing, nurturing, emotional and physical security, and to provide access to the wider environment so that they can learn about a variety of things. Some people (whether or not they are on the autism spectrum) love children, while others do not want anything to do with them. Children require such a large amount of energy from their parents that it is never a good idea just to have them because the person you are in a relationship with thinks that it would be a good idea.

You can choose whether or not to share a household with someone who has children, just as you can decide whether or not you want to have children. If you are unable to physically have children your decision may be around adoption, in vitro fertilization (IVF), surrogacy or co-parenting. Sometimes we decide one thing, but as life develops we change our mind or circumstances change making us more open to having or not having children.

> K.C.: I had my daughter quite young. She wasn't planned, I just wasn't even thinking about it. I had sex with a guy I met at uni, who told me he loved me and it would be nice. It was nice, but then I was pregnant and he was nowhere to be found. I didn't even realize I was pregnant for a few months as my periods were always very unpredictable and I didn't get morning sickness or anything. I love my daughter and I am OK at parenting, but I really struggled with the baby stage, all that poo and sick. Yuck, it just smells terrible, and she couldn't communicate with me yet. As she got older and we could communicate, it got easier. If I had my time again I would have made him wear a condom. I think I would have found life much easier without a child.

> Dean: My wife and I wanted children because we wanted to give a child a better life than we had as aspies growing up when the world did not understand. We planned our lives carefully but it took three years for her to get pregnant with our oldest, but only six months for the next one. Our third one is three years younger again. It was very overwhelming when we had three kids under five. But both of us love exploring the world with our kids, getting excited by looking for bugs in the garden or learning how to cook pancakes.

> Lucy: I had a relationship with a woman who had shared care of her son. But then things changed and we ended up with him all the time. I missed walking around naked as I had to wear clothes

when he was around. I lost my private time and space because our house wasn't big enough. He is a lovely boy and we get on fine but I miss my me time, my quiet space. Now I have to go and sit in the car to be alone, which is not perfect as it is cold in winter and hot in summer.

Different people will be impacted differently by children of any age. Some people believe that it is different if you are biologically the parent than if you are not, but for other people this is irrelevant.

Lucy: I remember my friend saying that I would never love my stepson properly because he wasn't my blood. I had no idea what she was talking about, I mean my partner is not my blood and we love each other just fine. My stepson and I love each other just fine too. Weird.

Tom: During an argument with my in-laws they said I wasn't blood related so my thoughts weren't valid. I found this so stupid, I mean they weren't blood related either, because that would be incest, which is illegal. I think it was meant to hurt my feelings but it just made me think they were illogical and were losing the argument.

Babies

Babies can be born to and stay with one or both of their birth parents, or they can be fostered or adopted. Some babies are conceived naturally, while others are conceived through IVF or other fertility procedures, surrogacy, donor eggs and/or sperm. Access to these types of procedures is governed by regulations that vary around the world. In many countries it can be very difficult to adopt a baby, as many people who do apply to adopt specify that they would prefer a baby to an older child.

After conception (when the sperm from a male fertilizes the egg from a female) the fertilized egg attaches itself to the uterus and starts to grow and develop inside the womb. More pregnancies end in miscarriage than give rise to live births, most before 12 weeks. This is why some people choose not to announce a pregnancy until 12 weeks. For some women, pregnancy is easy and they feel and look comfortable or even radiant, while for others it is a difficult and distressing time. If the foetus is miscarried, this can be a very difficult and sad time for the family. An additional difficulty for people who experience miscarriage, is that it is not talked about often.

Babies can be quiet and passive or very noisy with lots of energy, or anything inbetween. Many babies crave touch and like to be held. They recognize people by smell and then visually. Babies with face blindness will not recognize faces and may learn other clues like voice, hair, etc. Babies need to be interacted with when they are awake and given things to do and explore so that their brains develop. They often become the focus of their mother's attention and this can be difficult for some other family members. If the main carer of the baby is tired they may need extra help with household chores like cooking or cleaning. They may also lose interest in sex with their partner, or they may not.

Having the baby sleep in the same room as the mother can be helpful for breastfeeding on demand, though it is safer for the baby to sleep in their own cot or other bed to minimise the risk of sudden infant death syndrome. Some cultures make special sleeping baskets for babies, such as the Wahakura, a woven flax bassinette, used in New Zealand. If the baby sleeps in their parents' room some adults are uncomfortable with this and it can affect their relationship. Other adults see this as natural and do not have an issue with it. If the baby does not sleep much and/or cries a lot, this can cause sleep deprivation for the adults, which can also impact negatively on a relationship as stress increases.

Pregnancy

Pregnancy has a large effect not just on a woman's body, but also on her emotional state, no matter how the pregnancy has come about. Pregnancy can also impact on sexual desire, feelings of self-worth and self-image. These impacts are different for different people: while some women blossom during pregnancy, others can feel awful.

People often congratulate pregnant women on their pregnancy and, while this is appropriate in most cases, it may be upsetting for a mum-to-be who did not plan her pregnancy and is still unsure about whether or not she wants to be a mother. Some women are asked about due dates (when the baby is due to be born, which is approximately 40 weeks from conception) when they are not even pregnant, but have large bellies. This can cause great offence!

Seeing someone who is pregnant, if you really want a baby but have been unable to conceive or do not have a partner with whom to have a child, can be upsetting for some people. This seems to be partly due to human biology and the biological drive to reproduce, and individual desire to have a baby to 'complete themselves'.

Many medications are unsafe for mothers-to-be to take during pregnancy and, if you are a female who may conceive (i.e. you are engaging in heterosexual intercourse of penis into vagina), then you should discuss the safety of any medications you are taking with your doctor. Examples of unsafe medications are sodium valproate and thalidomide. If you have a mental illness and want to have a baby, you will need to work closely with your mental health team on how to achieve this while staying well.

The consumption of alcohol during pregnancy can severely affect the baby. It is unknown why some babies are affected and others appear not to be. There has not yet been enough research in this area to give any definitive answers on safe quantities of alcohol in pregnancy. Some women become pregnant when they are not actively trying to do so and do not always know that they have become pregnant for a few months. This is because, although most women's periods stop during pregnancy, there are some women who have some bleeding. During pregnancy all bleeding from the vagina should be medically evaluated as soon as possible.

Being pregnant causes a woman's body to change shape and size. She may feel more hungry or tired as well as needing to go to the toilet more frequently. Some women suffer from morning sickness, which is where they feel nauseous and vomit a lot during pregnancy. Morning sickness can occur at any time of the day or night and often resolves after 12–14 weeks of pregnancy, but can adversely affect some women for their whole pregnancy. Other physical health changes can occur and it is important to have regular checkups with your doctor.

Being on the autism spectrum as such will not affect a pregnancy, although it may affect your sensory sensitivities and food preferences as well as sleeping habits. However, experiencing birth may well be impacted by being on the autism spectrum. Attending prenatal classes and alerting your care team to your diagnosis and the way it affects you should help you to be prepared for the birth. You cannot tell at or just after birth if a child is or is not on the autism spectrum. The midwives or other health professionals will teach you how to breastfeed, change nappies and hold and bathe the baby safely. You may need to ask them to teach you this in a way that you learn best. You can get a friend or family member to write all the instructions down and/or take photos and then make a 'how to care for baby' book for you, if this would be useful.

It is usually fine to have sex during pregnancy and your doctor will tell you if there are any restrictions. Some women are very amorous and loving and want lots of sex during pregnancy and some do not want any sex at all.

Infants and toddlers

Infants and toddlers can be noisy, smelly, dirty, and require a lot of energy, attention and love. For some people caring for an infant or toddler is extremely rewarding and brings a great deal of joy and happiness to them; however, for others it can just be hard work and overwhelming from the perspectives of energy and emotions. Even though they are small, infants and toddlers can appear to take up a lot of space physically, especially once they start crawling/walking unaided.

Infancy is when children learn what communication is for and various different ways to communicate. It is also when children start to explore the wider environment and not just the immediately reachable vicinity. Once they start to crawl or walk (toddling is the unsteady walking that children do when they are learning to stand and move on their own two feet unaided), children explore everything. It is often at this stage that it becomes apparent whether a child is or is not on the autism spectrum. Autism has a large genetic component, but a child can have two parents on the autism spectrum and not be themselves, or they can be but neither parent is.

All infants and toddlers need to experience their environment, learn how to meet new people and handle new things. If this is very difficult for you, you could learn together. It is important not to anticipate all the needs and wants of young children, but to respond to their communication quickly so that they learn the point of communicating, which is to express needs and wants and convey information.

Between two and three years old most children go through a phase called the 'terrible twos', which is when they are developing a sense of themselves as separate entities from the other people in their life and starting to try to exert control over their environment. 'No' often becomes one of their favourite words to use and most hated words to hear. Seeking out other parents on the autism spectrum can be very useful at this stage to find out what strategies have worked for them in raising their children well in ways that are not overwhelming for them.

It can be very difficult to have uninterrupted adult time without infants and toddlers interrupting when they share a household. Some adults find this very stressful, and families where one or more people need quiet alone time in order to manage to live as well as possible need to work out how to facilitate this. Adults who spend time with a partner and their children of this age can find these children fun or intense and hard work. As children grow and become toilet trained, they move on from nappies to using the toilet but can still have 'accidents' where they wee or poo in their clothes. This can be overwhelming for some adults, especially if they are sensitive to smell or have issues around germs and cleanliness.

School age children

Children start school at different ages in different countries, with many children attending preschool too. If your child has any difficulties interacting with others or managing their behaviour in a socially acceptable way (in mainstream society) or has an autism spectrum diagnosis, seek out a school that has staff who understand the autism spectrum or are willing to learn from you. You may need to help teachers understand your child's potential, particularly if they start school non-verbal.

If you have a typical child, they may want to have things like birthday parties at home or to spend nights at their friends' houses or have sleepovers at home. All of these things can be quite disruptive, noisy and create a mess. However, typical children enjoy socializing and primary school is where they learn many social skills. If your child is part of a sports team or other out-of-school activity, you are expected to attend matches (to watch) or to offer to help out. If you are unable to due to other commitments such as caring for other children or working, it is helpful to make this clear in a calm way that expresses regret that you cannot be there (even if you are pleased about this).

All school age children require good nutrition, exercise and a reasonable amount of sleep in order to be able to learn at school. They also need to understand why they go to school and what the point of it is (to learn things so they can have a wider range of choices about how to live their lives when they are adults). They may require extra support at home if they struggle with some/all aspects of learning, or they may need to relax after school if they find it socially/emotionally overwhelming or just extremely tiring. There is no way to know in advance how your child will be and, if you have more than one child, regardless of their autism spectrum status, they are most likely to be completely different.

Children usually get homework from school and they are expected to do this, not you. Some children find school such an awful experience that their families choose to homeschool them. The laws on this vary from place to place. Some adults really enjoy homeschooling, while for others it is hard work and emotionally exhausting, so you need to be aware of your needs, strengths and limitations as well as your child's when thinking about this.

Children are often able to spend a reasonable amount of time engaged in their own activities, but they may want to get into bed with their parent(s) when they wake up. For some people involved in a relationship with a parent, they can find having children who are not their own in their bed really uncomfortable.

> Lucy: My partner and I were going on holiday and taking her son. When we looked at accommodation she wanted to get a family room because she said he wasn't old enough to have his own room. It was the most horrendous holiday for me because there was nowhere for me to just be as the room had two beds, the sofa, a kitchenette and a dining table all in the same room. There was a little bathroom too, but every time I went in there her son would want to go in, or in the mornings when I was desperate to pee, he would run in before me and then spend half an hour in there. The next year I said he had to have his own bedroom or I wouldn't go.

Another issue that can arise during the school years is the adult attitudes to education, nutrition, exercise and other lifestyle things. Where two adults disagree on fundamental aspects of child rearing it can lead to conflict, stress, distress and even arguments. It is better to agree to disagree or to discuss parenting styles and beliefs before having children.

Teenagers

Teenagers on the autism spectrum can be quite different from those who are not and, for children who have not previously been diagnosed, this can be when their differences become apparent, especially for girls. Puberty usually occurs during this phase and there will be a growing awareness of sexuality for many teens.

Typical teens can become very wrapped up in gender identity, sexuality and relationships, or very focused on their goals in life such as getting into a particular university. This is also the case for neurodiverse teens, although they are more likely to remain focused on their interests and passions and less on other people. However, teens on the autism spectrum who discover alcohol and/or drugs are very at risk of becoming regular users as they try to fit in with other people. At this age young people require a lot of parental input and guidance, though they may not appear to want or accept it.

Being non-judgemental but retaining firm boundaries with expectations of good behaviour is helpful in managing teens. Again, peer support for you as a parent is useful here, but if your teen is on the autism spectrum they can benefit hugely from peer support from other young people on the spectrum.

Teenagers tend to go to bed later and like to sleep later in the mornings, making it hard to get them up and ready for school on time, which can create a very stressful home environment. Teenagers should be encouraged to be responsible for their own behaviour and contribute to the household constructively. The adults in the household need to agree on a strategy, as typical teens are brilliant at playing one adult off against another to get their own way.

Access to the internet and time spent online are two areas of parenting that can create a lot of conflict between the teen and the adults in the house and between the adults. For some adults, the need for quiet time can become heightened as, although many teens communicate less, they can be intensely emotional and highly reactive, which can be exhausting for adults around them.

Adult children

Adult children, whether they are autistic or not, should be encouraged to be as independent as possible, although they may require financial, practical and/or emotional support from their parents at various times throughout life. If you have encouraged your teen to become more independent, this will transfer into adulthood. If, however, you have not enabled your teen to learn skills such as preparing simple meals, recognizing money, etc. you will need to do this before your adult child can successfully manage on their own or in a houseshare-type living arrangement.

Some adult children will require ongoing care of one kind or another, and may be dependent physically. This does not take away their rights to self-determination and choice over things in their life. Some residential service providers are excellent and others are certainly not. If an adult child requires this level of care they should be involved in the decision-making process.

Parents of adult children or adults involved in relationships with these parents may have very different ideas about the rights and responsibilities of the parents and of the adult children, and this can also cause a lot of conflict and arguments.

> Lynne: Once my stepson was an adult I thought we would not have to support him financially anymore because he did get a job, but my wife just kept on wanting to help him out all the time. I could either argue about it and end up upsetting both of us, or ignore it and fixate on it at night and not be able to sleep properly for weeks. Learning mindfulness has helped me with this, but I think my autistic logical mind finds all kinds of logical reasons why it is wrong and then I easily get fixated again.

> Wendy: My daughter wanted to stay at school for an extra year to get enough qualifications to go to university, and my partner was a bit disappointed because she had been looking forward

to my daughter leaving home so we could have our own space. She said she had been waiting four years for our own space, which really hurt my feelings: my daughter is an important part of my life and it is not like she won't exist when she moves out. I decided to try to understand exactly what my partner meant, and it turned out that, for him, when someone is not right then it is almost as if they don't exist, which is why I am the one who always calls his mother, because he just doesn't think to.

19

Choosing Not to Have Children

It is OK not to want children of your own, or to have children in the house you live in. If you feel this way and your partner agrees with you, this is an easy choice. However, if you do not want children but your partner does, this can mean the end of the relationship. Never lie to your partner in the hope that they will change their mind. Heterosexual couples are often expected by other family members to have children. Non-heterosexual couples do not usually have the same expectations imposed on them.

If you do not want to live in a house with children and you meet someone who you would like to have a long-term sexual relationship with, you need to find out if they have children. It is OK to ask people who you have just met if they have children. If they say yes, you should ask how old they are. Do not just turn around and walk off, as this will be seen as very rude.

You can have a sexual relationship with someone and yet both live in your own houses. However, if you do not want children and they have children, this is unlikely to work. People who are parenting alone (single parents) often need to prioritize their children over sexual relationships. If you meet a pregnant woman, she will soon become a mother so, if you do not like children, it would be unwise to become sexually involved.

If you meet an adult and they ask if you have children, you can simply say 'no I don't'. It is perceived as quite odd to add 'and I never want any'. You could however say, 'I enjoy being child free', and this is quite socially acceptable. If you do not want children and are medically unable to have children, it is OK to say, 'no I don't, I can't have kids'. Some people will respond to this in an emotional manner. Many people find it sad if someone is unable to have children. They may say something like, 'oh, I'm sorry'. A polite response to this is 'thanks'.

Some people may find out that you do not want to have children and they may want to know why. You do not have to explain why, no matter how often they ask. If you do want to explain, they may want to try to persuade you that you should have children. It would be unwise to have a sexual relationship with someone like this as they will continually try to persuade you even though you have been honest.

> Faith: I never wanted children and I had the perfect relationship for a number of years with this really great guy who seemed to understand me perfectly and we had such fun together. Then after a couple of years he started talking about wanting children and asking if I wanted to try to make a baby. I was so cross with him, I have no idea why he thought I would change my mind. Why would I want screaming, crying and dirty nappies? I wanted to say, would you like me to make you a gingerbread baby, like a gingerbread man cookie, but I didn't think he would see the humour. Instead we broke up. I have never found anyone I am as comfortable with but I couldn't share his vision for our

future and it would have been wrong of me to pretend I could. He is married with kids now, we are friends on Facebook but that's all.

Jo: I have mental health issues as well as autism and the medication I take can damage a baby so I would have to stop taking my medication if I wanted a baby, and whenever I try to stop I end up in hospital with a mental health crisis, so it's not worth it for me. I don't need a baby to complete my life; I am quite happy without one and now my husband sees how expensive kids are for his friends, so he is finally OK with it.

Greg: I asked my GP if I could have a vasectomy when I was still a teenager. I have always known I don't want children. The GP said no because 'you might change your mind'. More than 20 years later I haven't changed my mind. I don't know why it is hard for some people to believe or accept that someone can never want children.

For some women the choice to have children is not one that they realize they can make, instead some women just assume that it is a part of life, if they can find a partner. If you, or you and your partner, have never discussed the pros and cons of having children, it is a good idea to do so. In times gone by it was thought that having children would bring a couple closer together, but it is now known that this is rubbish! Children are expensive and hard work, and for some people this is enough of a reason to decide not to have them. For other people, the reasons not to have children relate to their own sensory issues, whereby the presence of a child would just be too overwhelming. Alternatively, for some people, the risks to the baby during pregnancy from the medications that they require to live well, such as sodium valproate, are too great. For these women, discussions with their clinicians should take place to look at alternative medications if there is any possibility for or desire to have a child.

A pros and cons list is really easy to make and should involve all the adults in the relationship, an example is given in Table 19.1:

Table 19.1 Pros and cons of having children

	Pros – reasons to decide to try to have children	Cons – reasons to decide not to have children
Carrie	I like being around children at my sister's house. I like the idea of being called Mum.	I like to have peace and quiet in the mornings. I hate the smell of nappies. I dislike pain intensely and worry about childbirth. We struggle financially already and a child would mean that we would really have problems with money.
Chris		I like living with Carrie and just Carrie.

These lists are very personal and may change over time. If one of you is more interested in having children than the other, you could revisit the list every six months or so. Men can produce sperm that are capable of creating life until they are quite old, whereas women's eggs become less viable with age, which means they are less likely to become pregnant and less likely to carry the baby to full term and have a live birth as they get older. A woman over 35 is medically viewed as an older mother and can be more at risk of complications for the baby during pregnancy and childbirth.

However, older mothers tend to be more financially stable, which can reduce financial stress on new families. They may also have a larger support network of friends and family who are willing and able to help out.

20

Physical and Mental Health and Relationships

Relationships can be positive, negative or neutral. In a neutral relationship your physical and/or mental health will not be affected. A positive relationship can improve your physical and/or mental health. If you have a medical condition, sometimes your health can get worse even in a very supportive relationship. This does not mean your relationship is bad, it means that you have a health problem that needs treatment.

In a negative relationship, your physical and/or mental health can get worse. It can be very hard to understand the difference between a good and bad relationship for anyone. If you do not have many friends or have not experienced any good relationships previously, it can be extremely difficult. Just because someone says they love you does not mean that they will take good care of you. In a good relationship the person is kind in their words and their actions. Arguing is a part of most relationships, but it should be brief and occur much less frequently than conversations that are not arguing.

Sadly some people hurt other people and this can also occur in relationships, whether or not the relationships are sexual. Both words and actual physical violence can be used. Physical violence can never be justified and is against the law. If someone with whom you have any kind of relationship hits you or otherwise hurts you physically, you must end the relationship with them and report it to the police. Even if the person who hit you says it is your fault or that they are very sorry, you must leave. It is very hard to leave someone you love, but if someone can injure you, they do not love you.

> Tara: I didn't know that lesbians could be violent, I knew that when a man hit his wife it was called domestic violence and that was really bad. I knew that you should leave as soon as you can after the first time they hit you, but I didn't because I thought that only applied to heterosexual relationships. After a while, someone at work asked if I was OK because I had some bruises on me. Because of my poor spatial awareness I often walk into doors. So, I told the person I had walked into a door. They said if I needed any help to let them know. It wasn't until years later that I understood battered women say they have walked into a door or fallen downstairs when they have been hurt by their partner. It was even harder to accept that I was a battered woman. I felt so stupid because I didn't know how it got from that first hit to being yelled at and her being mean all the time and hurting me physically more and more. I still don't know how I would have left if she hadn't thrown me out because she found someone she liked more. Luckily I had some friends and I lived in their spare room until I felt better. I left with one small bag of clothes and photos, she kept everything else because she said it was hers not mine.

It is important not to believe someone if they say it is your fault that they were mean or violent to you. If you are mean or violent to someone that you spend time with, you need to go and get counselling to manage your feelings more safely. It is *not* OK to hurt others. The only exception is if you are being hurt and you need to hurt them back to get away. In this case you *must* go straight to the police or a hospital and report what has just happened.

If you become depressed in a relationship, it is not necessarily the relationship that is causing the depression. If your partner suggests that you are depressed, or you feel you might be depressed, make an appointment to see your family doctor and take a list with you that explains why you feel you might be depressed. Your family doctor may prescribe medication and/or talk therapy or they may refer you to a psychologist or psychiatrist for an assessment. It is important to note that many adults on the autism spectrum have atypical reactions to medications used to treat depression, anxiety and other mental health issues. You may need very small amounts or larger doses than other people, and it may be less of one thing and more of another. You will need to ask the doctor who writes your prescription to explain clearly how you will know it is working or, if the dose is too large or small, what that might feel like to you or look like to your friends and family.

21

Physical and Mental Health and Sexual Activity

Just like we can have things go wrong with our bodies and we call these diseases or viruses, etc., we can get sexually transmittable infections (STIs) if the person (people) we engage in sexual activity with already has these STIs. You cannot always see if someone has an STI and many people do not know they are infected or choose to not tell others. In addition, if you engage in penetrative heterosexual sex the woman may get pregnant.

Safe sex is the term for using strategies to prevent the transmission of STIs such as HIV/AIDS, and to prevent pregnancy where relevant. For men, this involves wearing a condom. Condoms are not easy to put on your or someone else's penis unless you have had practice. You may want to practise on a banana if you are a female. Men can practise on their own penis! Condoms can sometimes be obtained free at sexual health clinics or doctors' offices. Otherwise you will need to buy them – because some people steal condoms, they are often kept behind the counter at the drug store and you have to ask for them. Do not be embarrassed, it is OK to ask for condoms. You can ask for them in a number of ways as there are lots of different types and brands. They are sold in boxes. Another way to buy condoms is from vending machines in bars/clubs – these are usually in the toilets.

When you open the box, there are a number of packets inside. Each packet contains a condom. Condoms can only be used once and must be thrown away after use. *Never* agree to have sex without a condom with someone you have not got a committed relationship with. New cases of HIV infection are increasing as young people do not realize how prevalent the virus is. HIV is not just in the gay community, women can be infected by men and vice versa. Transmission between lesbians is very rare, but some lesbians choose to use gloves or latex barriers called dental dams when touching vaginas with their hands or mouths. Dental dams should be used for oral sex only, as they are not effective protection for anal or vaginal sex.

Some men will try to persuade you to have sex without them using a condom because 'it feels so much better'. Even if this is true – tough! Many STDs have very serious side effects and require medical treatment.

Other things men will say to try to get you to have sex without a condom are:

▶ If you really loved me you would.

▶ If you trusted me you would.

▶ I'll pull out in time (to prevent sperm entering the vagina and possibly causing pregnancy).

▶ I don't have a condom with me, and I really want to do it now.

- ▶ I can't wait.

- ▶ I've been tested and I'm fine (this is claiming they have no STDs or HIV).

- ▶ It's against my religion (where this is true it is also against their religion to be having sex outside of marriage).

In any of these situations, it is important to say no and, if they keep asking, desexualize the situation. You can do this by putting your clothes back on, going to the bathroom or asking if the man would like a cup of tea or a drink. If you say no but you have some condoms, you can offer to put it on for them and often the man will be happy with this. In general men would prefer to have sex with a condom than not have sex at all.

Condoms are only effective if they are used correctly. To ensure your condoms will work you need to ensure they have not expired (check the date on the packet). Condoms should not be removed from their packets until you are about to use them. They need to be kept in a cool, dry place and not in direct sunlight. When you take it out of the packet you need to check it only has the large hole for the penis to enter and no other holes. If you are going to be using a lubricant with the condom it needs to be water based, like KY jelly, which you can buy in drug stores/pharmacies. If you use massage oils, baby oil or Vaseline, these can cause the condom to break. Both condoms and dental dams can only be used once and should be safely disposed of in a rubbish bin after use and not left on the floor. Men may wish to take their used condoms home with them to throw away to make sure it is actually thrown away.

Women who want to decrease their likelihood of getting pregnant may want to discuss other forms of contraception with their family doctor. There are a number of options that can be considered, though it does need to be remembered that these options do not protect against sexually transmitted diseases or infections. Some of these options are contraceptive tablets, commonly known as 'the pill', emergency contraception tablets – the availability of which varies from place to place, contraceptive implants and injections, intrauterine devices (often referred to as IUDs), which can be either copper or hormonal, vaginal rings, barrier methods (male and female condoms and diaphragms) and also sterilization – of the woman and/or her partner. Women who have had hysterectomies cannot get pregnant.

Contraception can have side effects, so it is important to discuss your personal options with a doctor or sexual health/ family planning nurse. Urban myths suggest that a woman cannot get pregnant if she has sex standing up (UNTRUE), or the first time she has sex (again UNTRUE). Women cannot get pregnant from anal intercourse but some women do not like the idea or the actuality of this type of sexual activity, so it may not be something that is an option for you or your partner(s).

STIs include genital herpes, chlamydia, syphilis, gonorrhea, scabies, pubic lice (crabs), hepatitis and HIV (the virus that causes AIDS). These are explained below.

Genital herpes

Genital herpes is caused by the herpes simplex virus (HSV1 or HSV2). HSV1 more often occurs around the mouth, but it can also occur on the genitals, whereas HSV2 usually occurs on and around the genital area. There are reports that about 12 per cent of adults have the herpes simplex virus and about 80 per cent of infected adults are unaware that they have this infection. It is difficult to know when a person first becomes infected with the herpes simplex virus as it can take weeks to years for any signs and symptoms to show, if they ever do.

Path of infection

The herpes simplex virus is spread by skin-to-skin contact and so can infect someone during vaginal, oral or anal sex. Cold sores on the mouth can cause genital infection during oral sex. Pregnant women with genital herpes should tell their antenatal care provider as, very rarely, herpes infection can be transmitted to their baby during delivery, which can lead to complications for their baby.

Signs and symptoms

There can be no signs and symptoms of herpes for days, weeks, months or years or ever. However, for some people herpes can cause considerable pain and distress. Symptoms may include:

- ▶ flu-like symptoms including headaches and pains in the back and legs

- ▶ enlarged glands in the groin

- ▶ small blisters around the genitals – these break open to form shallow, painful ulcers, which scab over and heal after one to two weeks

- ▶ small cracks in the skin with or without an itch or tingling

- ▶ redness or a distinct rash

- ▶ considerable pain and swelling in the genital area, and may have additional pain and difficulty passing urine.

Not everyone will experience all or indeed any of these symptoms.

Treatments

There is no cure for the herpes virus. Treatment is aimed at reducing symptoms and decreasing the frequency of further outbreaks of symptoms. Symptoms can be improved by:

- ▶ salt baths

- ▶ ice packs to the affected area

- ▶ pain-relieving medicines like paracetamol

- ▶ antiviral medications like acyclovir, famciclovir and valaciclovir.

These medications are most effective if used as soon as you become aware of any symptoms appearing. Please note that topical antivirals usually used for cold sores on the lips or face are not appropriate for use on the genitals.

Chlamydia

Chlamydia is caused by the bacterium *Chlamydia trachomatis* and is one of the most common STIs. It can affect women and men of all ages, but is most common in people who are under 25 years of age. Chlamydia can be present with no signs or symptoms but, left untreated, it can cause a number of problems including pelvic inflammatory disease (PID). Symptoms of PID include: lower abdominal pain and tenderness, deep pain during sexual intercourse, heavy and painful periods and fever.

Path of infection

Chlamydia is spread by unprotected vaginal or anal sex with an infected person. In men, chlamydia infects the urethra and may spread to the tube that carries sperm from the testicles (the epididymis). In women, chlamydia can infect the cervix and spread to the uterus and fallopian tubes, causing pelvic inflammatory disease (PID), chronic pelvic pain and infertility. If a pregnant woman has chlamydia, it can be passed on to her baby during birth, causing lung or eye infections.

You can get chlamydia and other STIs from a new sexual partner who has had sex with an earlier infected partner. It can also be spread from a long-term partner who has unprotected sex with other people. Because most people do not know whether or not they have chlamydia, if you are sexually active it is important to have an annual chlamydia checkup.

Signs and symptoms

Men who have chlamydia usually don't have any signs or symptoms. In men, if symptoms are present, they may include:

▶ a discharge from the penis

▶ discomfort when urinating

▶ swollen and sore testes.

Most women who are infected have no signs or symptoms of chlamydia. In women, if symptoms are present, they may include:

▶ an unusual vaginal discharge

▶ a burning feeling when urinating

▶ pain during sex

▶ bleeding or spotting between periods or bleeding after sex

▶ lower abdominal pain.

Treatments

If detected early, chlamydia can be treated with a single dose of antibiotics. If complications from chlamydia infection have already developed, such as pelvic inflammatory disease in women, this will require you to take a longer course of antibiotics.

If you find out that you have chlamydia, you or your doctor will need to inform your sexual partner(s) so that they can be tested and treated, as they may be infected and can infect you again after treatment. You should have another test for chlamydia three months after you are treated.

Syphilis

Syphilis is an STI caused by a bacterium called *Treponema pallidum*. It can affect both men and women. Syphilis is transmitted through close skin-to-skin contact and is highly contagious when the syphilis sore, known as a chancre or a syphilitic rash, is present. There are higher rates of syphilis in different countries: in some countries men who have sex with men are at a higher risk of becoming infected with syphilis than other people.

Early treatment is very effective; however, as some people may not have any symptoms or signs of early syphilis, it can develop and be more difficult to treat. This is why sexual health checkups are recommended every three to six months depending on your sexual activities and types of partners. Left untreated, long-term syphilis can be fatal or may lead to chronic brain or heart disease. Syphilis testing is always done as part of routine antenatal screening when a woman is pregnant.

Path of infection

Syphilis is transmitted through skin-to-skin contact and therefore oral, vaginal or anal sex with a person who has recently become infected can infect you. Syphilis can also be transmitted from a mother to her baby during pregnancy and at birth. This is called congenital syphilis and is relatively rare. The incubation time for syphilis is between ten days and three months.

Signs and symptoms

There are three stages of syphilis. Only the first two stages are infectious and symptoms vary according to the stage. Having symptoms of syphilis can make you more at risk of HIV infection during sexual contact.

SYMPTOMS IN FIRST STAGE OF SYPHILIS
(4 TO 12 WEEKS)

There may be no symptoms, or there may be an ulcer on the penis or vagina, or genital area or anus, or the mouth. You may not be able to see the ulcer if it is in the rectum or on the cervix. The sore is normally painless and usually occurs any time between 1 and 12 weeks after infection. The sore usually heals completely within 4 weeks. If left untreated at this stage, the person may go on to develop the second stage of the disease.

SYMPTOMS IN SECOND STAGE OF SYPHILIS
(UP TO 24 MONTHS)

A flat, red skin rash on the soles of the feet or palms of the hands, or it may cover the entire body. The rash is contagious and may mimic other common skin conditions such as measles. The diagnosis may be missed if a syphilis blood test is not done. Other symptoms that may occur are:

▶ swollen lymph nodes

▶ hair loss

▶ joint pain

▶ a flu-like illness.

If you are infected with syphilis and do not seek treatment at this stage, you may develop the third stage of the infection.

THIRD STAGE OF SYPHILIS (5 TO 20 YEARS AFTER THE INITIAL INFECTION)

Various organs can be affected, with severe brain and heart complications in about one-third of untreated people. Syphilis is not infectious at this point and is still treatable.

Congenital syphilis

Infants born with congenital syphilis may have no symptoms at birth. Early congenital syphilis may include symptoms such as a runny nose, sore on the skin, bone abnormalities, eye, liver or kidney problems. Late congenital syphilis, which presents after two years of age, may present with skeletal problems, dental defects, eye problems and deafness.

Treatments

Penicillin is an effective treatment for all stages of syphilis, including congenital syphilis. If you are allergic to penicillin, you may be able to undergo a procedure that safely allows you to be given penicillin or given a different antibiotic.

Gonorrhoea (the clap)

Gonorrhoea is caused by a bacterium known as *Neisseria gonorrhoeae*. It usually affects the genital area, although the throat or anus (back passage) may also be involved. If left untreated in women, gonorrhoea can lead to PID, which can cause infertility. Gonorrhoea is sometimes known as the clap.

Path of infection

Gonorrhoea affects both men and women and is easily transmitted during vaginal intercourse. It can also be transmitted during anal or oral sex.

Signs and symptoms

A small percentage of men have no symptoms at all. Gonorrhoea usually infects the urethra. Symptoms may include:

▶ a burning sensation while urinating or passing water

▶ a white or yellow pus-like discharge from the penis

▶ swelling and pain in the testicles, which can occur if the gonorrhoea infection goes untreated.

Often women have no symptoms. Sometimes, gonorrhoea causes:

▶ an unusual discharge from the vagina

▶ pain while urinating.

Women who have had PID need regular screening for gonorrhoea, because the risk of infertility increases with each bout of inflammation caused by the gonorrhoea.

Treatments

Gonorrhoea is treated with antibiotics; however, some strains of gonorrhoea are now resistant to penicillin and some other antibiotics. Tell your doctor if you have been travelling overseas because this may affect the antibiotic chosen to treat your gonorrhoea.

Scabies

Scabies is an infestation of skin caused by very small mites called *Sarcoptes scabiei*. The mites burrow into the skin to lay their eggs, which then hatch into new insects. Scratching can spread the infestation even more. Scabies is very common around the world and can affect anyone. Pets can have scabies but this is different to, and does not cause, human scabies infections. If you develop scabies, your sexual partners and all members of your household will also need to be treated.

Path of infection

Scabies is spread by direct, prolonged physical contact including sexual activity. However, scabies mites can survive away from humans for up to 36 hours, so it is possible to get scabies from infected articles such as bed linen and clothing, although this is less common.

Signs and symptoms

The main symptoms of scabies are:

▶ intense itching, usually worse after a hot bath or shower and at night

▶ visible burrows on the skin between the fingers and in skin creases like the armpits and genitals

▶ a bump or pimple-like rash, which is often difficult to see

▶ small, clear, fluid-filled spots or lesions.

Treatments

Treatment involves applying a cream or lotion specifically used for treating scabies to your whole body from the chin down avoiding your eyes, nose and mouth. The treatment may need to be repeated in one week's time to kill recently hatched mites. If the pimples or spots become infected, antibiotics may be necessary. Treatment may vary and your doctor will need to tell you which treatment is best for you. The itch may persist for two to three weeks after treatment, even if the scabies have been effectively treated. This is because the itch is caused by the body's immune system responding to the mites and may take time to settle down. You can talk to your pharmacist about treatments available to help with the itch.

In addition any clothing, bedding or towels used in the last two or three days should be washed on a hot cycle or dry-cleaned to kill any mites that are on them.

Pubic lice (crabs)

Pubic lice is an infection of *Phthirus pubis* lice, which is often nicknamed crabs. The infestation can be found in pubic hair and sometimes also in the hair of the armpit, eyebrows, eyelashes, beard and torso. Pubic lice are small, flat, light-brown parasites that cling to pubic hair and suck blood for nourishment. Blood sucking from pubic lice can cause small red areas or sores and itching. Lice infestation causes no serious harm, but can be irritating. If you have pubic lice, you may want to get tested for other STIs just in case. Head lice are not the same as pubic lice.

Path of infection

Pubic lice are usually transmitted through direct skin-to-skin contact, including sexual activity. However, they can also be spread by contact with towels, or the underwear or bedding of an infected person.

Signs and symptoms

Some people have no symptoms and may be unaware of the lice infestation. However, for others the main symptom is itching of the affected area. This is often worse at night. Lice and nits (eggs from the lice) can sometimes be seen, especially stuck to the pubic hairs.

Treatments

Topical creams or lotions containing permethrin need to be applied to the affected area and this is the most commonly recommended treatment. See your doctor, pharmacist or sexual health centre for further advice. Permethrin should not be applied to the eyelashes. If this area is affected, discuss an alternative treatment with your doctor.

Hepatitis

There are three forms of hepatitis (hep), hepA, hepB and hepC, each of which is caused by a virus of the same name (i.e. the hepatitis A virus causes hepA). All three types of hepatitis are liver illnesses; the hepA virus usually makes people sick for only one to three weeks, whereas the hepC virus causes a life-long illness. HepB affects different people differently, with adults usually fine after clearing the virus, whereas children and babies infected with hepB can have life-long liver problems, including cancer of the liver. Although most adults recover from hepB, it can lead to serious illness or death in some people. Immunization is the best protection against hepB infection.

Path of infection

The hepB virus is carried in blood and in lesser quantities in vaginal fluid and semen. You can get hepB by having unsafe sex, sharing needles for piercing, drug use or tattoos. The virus may also be passed from a pregnant mother to her baby. In some cases infections occur without a known cause.

Signs and symptoms

Some people who are infected with the hepB virus have mild, flu-like symptoms and some do not become sick at all.

In more severe cases, hepB can cause:

▶ loss of appetite

▶ nausea and vomiting

▶ pain in the liver, which is under the right ribcage

▶ fever

▶ pain in the joints

▶ jaundice.

Usually these symptoms disappear in a few weeks but even when the person is feeling better they can still be infectious. Most adults who become infected with the hepB virus recover completely and do not become infected again. A few people become very ill and some may even die.

Complications of hepB

A small percentage of people who become infected with the hepB virus develop a long-term hepB infection. A person with long-term hepB is at risk of developing chronic liver disease or liver cancer later in life.

Treatments

Most adults who become infected with hepB will clear the infection by themselves if their immune system is healthy. These people may not need any treatment. However adults with long-term hepB require long-term treatment to help clear the virus and reduce liver damage. Current treatments for this include antiviral medications. It is important to avoid drinking alcohol if you have liver disease.

HIV and AIDS

The human immunodeficiency virus (HIV) weakens the immune system and causes acquired immune deficiency syndrome (AIDS). It can take many years for someone who has the HIV virus to develop AIDS. When the immune system is weakened, various infections and cancers are more easily able to affect the person with AIDS. Early testing for HIV helps people to stay healthy and reduces the spread of the infection in the community. There is no vaccine or cure for HIV or AIDS, but life-long medication can manage HIV-related illnesses and AIDS. Someone who has the HIV virus is said to be HIV positive, and this is often written as HIV+. HIV affects both men and women, and the best protection against acquiring HIV is to practise safe sex and not to put bodily fluids from someone else into your body.

A blood test can detect HIV antibodies and tell if you are infected with the virus. For up to 12 weeks after you have been infected the antibodies against HIV can't be detected in the blood, so you may need to have a second test three months after a negative test. If your blood test shows that antibodies are present, you are infected with HIV.

Path of infection

HIV is spread in a number of ways including having sex without a condom, and sharing needles and other injecting equipment. You have a risk of being infected with HIV even if you participate in a high-risk activity like sharing needles or having unsafe sex only once. Practising safe sex reduces the risk of infection and is vital if either partner has HIV or if either partner is unsure whether they have HIV. Safe sex means sex where semen, vaginal secretions or blood are not exchanged between sexual partners. Using condoms and water-based lubricants during vaginal or anal sex greatly reduces the risk of infection.

Signs and symptoms

HIV does not have symptoms that are the same for every person infected. In addition most symptoms of HIV are the same as those experienced in a variety of other illnesses. However, if you think you have been put at risk of getting HIV, or if you have any of the signs below (or a combination of them) for longer than about a month you should consult your doctor. Symptoms can include:

- ▶ flu-like symptoms

- ▶ extreme and constant tiredness

- ▶ fevers, chills and night sweats

- ▶ rapid weight loss for no known reason

- ▶ swollen lymph glands in the neck, underarm or groin area

- ▶ white spots or unusual marks in the mouth

- ▶ skin marks or bumps, either raised or flat, usually painless and purplish

- ▶ continuous coughing or a dry cough

- ▶ diarrhoea

- ▶ decreased appetite.

Treatments

Treatment is required for life and is specific to each individual, with most people taking a large number of different medications, sometimes called a cocktail of drugs. AIDS is incurable and the treatments enable people to live longer and more healthily than they would be able to otherwise.

As can be seen, there are a number of physical health issues that can arise if people engage in unprotected or unsafe sex. Using condoms can prevent all of the STIs above except pubic lice and scabies as they live in the pubic hair, which is not covered by a condom. The other reason that some people choose to use condoms when engaging in heterosexual sex is to prevent pregnancy.

Pregnancy can also be prevented with other contraceptives, though it should be noted that no contraception is 100% effective. Some contraceptives are tablets that the woman needs to take every day, others are injections, transdermal patches or intrauterine devices. Women need to discuss contraception with their family doctor or gynaecologist as there are risks and benefits from each type.

If you are sexually active, every 6 to 12 months you should ask your doctor or family planning clinic for a full sexual health screen. This will consist of a physical examination of your genitals, and blood tests. Women will also have a pap smear test, which involves a cell sample being taken from the cervix to test for cervical cancer. It is a good idea for women to ask for a physical breast examination too. This checks for early signs of breast cancer.

Even if you stay in good physical health you may struggle with mental health issues, as many adults on the autism spectrum do. For some people sexual activity can trigger mental health issues if they have been a victim of sexual abuse or violence previously. Sexual activity in itself should not be a negative experience if it is consensual. However, if you find some aspects very distressing or uncomfortable and are unable to explain this to your partner(s), you may develop some anxiety or stress around sexual activity and sexual relationships. In this case it would be useful to find other adults on the spectrum with similar experiences to find out their experiences. In addition you may choose to talk to a counsellor or psychologist. It is important that you find someone who understands the autism spectrum and has experience of sexual relationship counselling as these are both specialist fields.

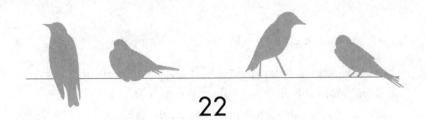

22

Summary

Autistic spectrum adults can enjoy a wide range of relationships no matter how much they struggled with relationships as a child. Healthy relationships are rewarding and can bring joy and happiness; however, they are also hard work to maintain long term, no matter what type of relationship it is. Working on a relationship starts when the people involved want to maintain their relationship in a positive way, and have a commitment to do so.

Keys to successful relationships are:

▶ accepting and understanding yourself

▶ being kind and caring towards yourself and the people that you are in relationships with

▶ learning what kind of relationships you want and how to go about finding and maintaining these relationships

▶ getting peer support from other autism spectrum adults on how to find and maintain positive relationships

> ▶ seeking help to end unhealthy relationships.

Sexuality and gender are more fluid that traditional society suggests and it is fine to explore your identities and desires by yourself or in consensual and respectful relationships. Consent:

> ▶ should always be discussed

> ▶ can be withdrawn at any time and this *must* be respected

> ▶ is not a given or a right, it is a gift that must be respected by both / all parties.

Sexual activity should be fun and pleasurable and take place alone or with consenting partner(s) in a safe place and manner. In many countries this means that sexual activity can only take place in private places and not in public. You do not have to engage in any sexual activities if you do not want to, it is not better or worse to be sexual or non-sexual – it just is.

INDEX